Black Folks Don't Tip

Black Folks Don't Tip

Exploring the African-American Dining Phenomenon

Kassondra Rockswell

Cover Design by Planet Rockswell

Published by Balance Books

for

AlmaRose Sovereign Voice GoldenHeart Teacher

I thought I was just raising you…
I had no clue you were raising me too

SERVER SALUTATION

for all the masters of menus
in mismanaged venues
ever-persistent souls
in penguin-suits, aprons and oil resistant soles
like magicians and clowns under a circus tent
trying to make a dollar out of fifteen cents
juggling rules that make no sense
with no financial recompense
underappreciated and underpaid
like an antebellum southern negro maid
marching through backdoors
sweeping and mopping floors
high-volume, fast paces
in the broken bowels and dank basements
of otherwise immaculate places

for the cleaning, the bussing, the wiping
the endless card swiping
and even more so
for your poor torso
with persistent burning that lingers
from lime juice cracked fingers
stiff neck, legs weak
aching back, throbbing feet
brand new bunions
make you cry like onions
every muscle hurting
yet you must keep working

forced to listen to pricks
much dumber than you
and take orders from a bitch
much younger than you
disrespected and dismissed

by the patrons too
trying to hold and stick
to your self-respect like glue

for every time you held your tongue
for every time you cried
for every polished glass
for every windsor knot tied
for the double-shift days
for every mile you walk in the maze
you are absolutely amazing
in so many ways

for all that you are
for all that you do
you mystical, magical, multi-tasking motherfuckers
I salute you

AUTHOR STATEMENT OF INTENT

The ideas and words contained within this body of literary work are intended to educate and uplift any and every person who chooses to read its contents. However, it delves into some negative behavior and unflattering stereotypes of African-American people. In doing so, it is not intended to alienate anyone, nor discourage individual wholeness, nor lead anyone down a path of concentrated negative thought in any way. To the contrary, these destructive issues must be addressed to create the dialogue which must take place among the citizens of the world to advance changes for the better. The ultimate intention of this book is education and enlightenment, which can be achieved through self-realization and new ways of thinking, new ways of acting, new ways of being. It is my desire that, included within, there is enough laughter and optimism to keep you in or propel you into your uttermost happiest place.

TABLE OF CONTENTS

CHAPTER 4

BLACK FOLKS DON'T EVOLVE

EXPLORING STEREOTYPES

CHAPTER 5

BLACK FOLKS DON'T TIP

PREFACE

I am a rock star.

I moved to Atlanta with my daughter, Sovereign, in the summer of 2008 to propel myself further into the rock star kingdom. If you had asked me then to consider getting a job as a server, I would have laughed in your face. *Me? Cleaning up nasty plates? Wiping tables? Uh...no thank you. I'm a rock star.*

After a couple years of starving passed, it was clear that the rock star checks were not big enough to pay the bills. My daughter was getting older, and bigger. She and I could no longer share a veggie plate, and she was outgrowing the kid's meal. And, there was always a field trip or some event at her school that required money. I had to do something.

A had a good friend who was a server. She always had money, and she always wanted to go out and kick it. I would always refuse out of brokeness, and she would always offer to pay my way. I thought, *maybe I should seriously consider this server thing*. On a whim, I called a diner in Midtown Atlanta, and turned out, they were hiring. I went in for an interview and started the same weekend. I made over $300 in two nights. I was so ecstatic to have made that money in such a short time, and I had it in my hand—cash. Out of excitement, my daughter and I took cell phone pictures of the money in various configurations. We took pictures with the money stacked with the $50 bill on top. We took one of the money spread out like playing cards. We took several more with the money in our hands and still others with the money coming out of our pockets and sleeves. I had never made cash that fast. I felt the joy of a new stripper, first night on the job.

As it turned out, I was a natural at being a server. It was much the same like performing. The table was my audience for which I sang out beautiful descriptions of the menu. I then danced food back and forth between the kitchen and the dining room in such a way as to deliver a performance warranting a great tip. This job was perfect for somebody like me.

At some point I pondered, *Wow, if I can make $300 in a weekend, I wonder if I can make $300 in a day?* With this question in mind, I began to seek out serving positions in Atlanta's Buckhead neighborhood, where I thought $300 a day might be possible. I left the diner in Midtown and headed up north. I found a gig where I did make $300 a day, but it took me all day to do it. I had to work a double shift and would be at work 14, sometimes 16 hours to make $300. With the intent on working smarter (rather than harder), ultimately, I found another gig and went from making $300 a day to making more than $300 per shift. I made even more money—but working only 5 or 6 hours a day as opposed to 14. I realized that I was making more money working as a server than I had made at any other job I had ever had—including the corporate one with the private office and the personal expense account.

As I moved between different serving jobs, I also realized very quickly that there was something overwhelmingly peculiar about black people and the way we behave when we dine out. As I served day after day, night after night, evident patterns and stereotypes of black folks began to show themselves very clearly. No matter how well-dressed or how professional or how famous, just about all of us behaved the same way and tipped the same way. Through daily conversations at work with server co-workers, I realized how big a phenomenon the topic had become. We all—black and white—felt the same way about serving black people. Together, as a team, we would cringe when a group of black folks walked in. Then we would laugh at whichever server ended up having to serve them.

Later, I would go out to dinner with my daughter or with my own black friends and end up on the receiving end of this same ridiculous treatment. Here I was, a server myself, pocket full of money, ready to overtip whoever had the guts to be nice to me and my black party, and I could not get any good service, no matter where I went. I could see how the servers were hesitant to serve me because I was black, just like I had been when it was my turn. It was an inexplicable, vicious cycle that never ended.

Because I now had money to spend, I went out to eat often so that I could enjoy it. Evaluating myself at the table, I had to admit that I, too, had some dining issues. Before I had become a server, I was in fact that very person I didn't want to serve. I was apathetic towards the experience, expectant of bad service and hesitant to tip. Or, I just tipped how I felt that day. Or, I tipped with whatever change was left over from the bill. Becoming a server helped me understand how bad this was—how bad *I* was, how bad we were collectively—and how bad America needed to have this tipping conversation.

I was hit with the epiphany to write a book about it. The stereotype was clear in the American world that black folks did not tip. But, when the topic came up, there was only frustration—for everybody from black to white, from server to diner. There was no clarity, no understanding, no patience from anyone regarding the matter. At different restaurants where I worked, I repeatedly watched co-workers stomp around the back of the restaurant, completely distraught over the way a group of black diners had been treating them. I have seen some even cry beyond consolation. The black-folks-not-tipping thing was unchartered territory. It was a mysterious taboo island on which no one dared step foot. It was an unbroken-down phenomenon that desperately needed to be broke down. This inexplicable cycle, I wanted to explain. And so, I wrote this book.

All in all, I am always, first and foremost, a writer. No matter what situation I find myself in, I will ultimately end up writing about it. Might be a song, might be a poem. In this case, it is a book.

In the 6 years it has taken me to complete this book, I have never once wavered in my absolute knowing that it was meant for this book to be written, and it was meant for this book to written by me. As a black woman, a lover of blackness, born and raised in American poverty, educated in American public schools and universities, I am completely prepared to testify on behalf of all I claim herein.

I was still working as a server when I began to write this book. Interestingly, I attracted certain situations with circumstances that seemed to be sent divinely to me, just so that I could put them in this book. So, I have included some of those situations as real testaments to the truth of the tipping and behavior of my own people. Some are funny. Some are just downright shameful. Others are a little bit of both. All are completely true, and with a couple of exceptions, happened directly to me or directly with me.

Some of these truths are so sour that they simply can't be sugarcoated, so some may argue that this book is chock full of negative statements about black people. *I am black people.* I understand it may be difficult to accept some of our ugly truths. But regardless of how ugly, if they are indeed true, then it is what it is. What is, however, can be better. And we should be better. We should always be striving to be more, and to be better.

As a writer and artist, it is my obligation and duty to take my inspired thought and share it in such a way that makes our world a better place—even if just a little. This book was written from three very fortunate perspectives: the fine dining guest, the waitstaff server, and most importantly, the black person. I get it—from all three angles. As a dining guest, I understand what it feels like to be the black person at the table. I know the experience of being repeatedly ignored from restaurant to restaurant, seated in the worst sections, watching great service pass you by. I understand, all too well, the agony of having intentions to tip well, only to have the opportunity to do so stolen from you by a server who is guilty of racial profiling. As a server, I understand the pain of working all day and night under disorganized management with the uncertainty of unpredictable tip pay. And I understand what it feels like to be so disrespected by a restaurant guest that you contemplate doing physical harm to them. And laughably, I also know what it feels like to promise yourself to keep giving your best service to *that black table* despite the fact black people have been disrespecting you all day. As a black person, I have the privilege of understanding black behavior and the origins thereof. Having been black all my life, I understand why black folks do things the way we do. My blackness makes me sensitive to discrimination and empathetic for love and understanding among all people. Then finally, as a writer, I am able to step outside the boundaries of all these perspectives, and truly see the picture on the wall.

I am speaking to my people—about ourselves, to help us grow a better understanding of ourselves. I am speaking to all America—about ourselves, to help us shine a brighter, more unified light on ourselves. I am speaking to the rest of the world, to help them gain a smidgen of insight into how our intricate infrastructure of race and politics interjects itself into every aspect of American culture. I challenge black people to read this book, to acknowledge the truths herein, then elevate themselves to become fearless, fully-active participants in the energy exchange of the world. I challenge everyone else to realize that historical racist values are still volcanically active everywhere in this country, to acknowledge the role each individual plays in perpetuating the injustices and the stereotypes therein, then to elevate themselves to be advocates for equality and social change.

I ran across an interview created by the *Living Off Tips Campaign* from Restaurant Opportunities Centers United (ROCU) where Gloria Steinem so beautifully said,

> *There are people who care deeply about whether or not everything on their plate has been grown within a hundred miles, but do they care about the person who's serving? And the way that will happen is by each person who's had this experience telling their story. I don't know of any social justice movement that hasn't started that way.*

Courage gained from statements like this give me the strength to move these ideas forward—come what may.

KR
October 2020
Atlanta, GA, USA

INTRODUCTION

Yes, it is true. Black folks do not tip. Yes, there are exceptions to this statement. There are black people that tip, and there are other black people who tip well. However, exceptions of the latter are so few and far between that the black folks who actually do tip properly account for a very sad miniscule percentage of the African-American dining population. So few of us tip properly that it simply appears none of us tip at all.

The most apparent explanation as to why black folks do not tip is simple. Ignorance. Not ignorance meaning dumb or stupid, but ignorance defining a lack of knowledge. Black people do not tip because, for the most part, we simply do not know any better. We are ignorant of fine dining etiquette. When we dine out, most of us do not know what to do or how to do it. Quite frankly, since fighting for the civil human right to actually sit and dine inside the restaurant, rather than merely cleaning the restaurant, not much has changed in mass black culture regarding the understanding of proper dining etiquette. All we know is that we have the right to be there, so we show up. And we show up clueless about what is proper and what is unacceptable at the restaurant. This makes us awkward and uncomfortable.

What seems like merely food and drink to the uncultured diner goes far beyond what many of us can imagine. Fine dining restaurants have taken painstaking measures to offer dining guests the very best in food, flavor, ambience and service. The highest quality meats and freshest vegetables are acquired from local harvesters. Other international delicacies are flown in throughout the week to provide the ultimate feast options for the palate. The food is prepared and plated in such a way which decorates the table, to entice the eyes as well as the stomach. The servers are scrutinized daily for attire and knowledge, and they are educated daily with menu updates for food and beverage changes. To those who understand and appreciate this, going out to dinner is not simply eating something that tastes good. It represents having a wonderful experience, the creation of memories, the sharing of life with family and friends. Many who choose fine dining as a regular dining option understand and prefer this high standard in food and service. This is why they continuously return. They appreciate the attention to detail, the beautiful plating of the food and the immaculate server attire. All this beauty serves as a colorful backdrop to the stories of their lives. When we go to the restaurant without any understanding or appreciation of these things, with no respect of the etiquette already in place, we walk in destined to have an inferior dining experience.

For some, the word etiquette brings to mind aristocratic thoughts of napkins in laps and elbows off tables, but this is not the type of etiquette being referred to here. In this day and age, no one at the restaurant really cares about where you put your elbows. In this book, the reference to proper dining etiquette identifies the simple tools required to receive and enjoy a fine dining experience. Simple tools such as understanding the menu, placing an order, communicating with the server, and yes, tipping properly are all required to help enjoy a wonderful meal and create a memorable experience.

As a server, I quickly realized that most black people are not equipped with even the most basic knowledge of how to behave in a nice restaurant. The combination of black folks and restaurants is like oil and water--they just don't mix. Many times, we come to the table with a bad attitude. We have respect for neither the restaurant, nor the server. We are overbearing and inconsiderate.

We are unnecessarily aggressive. We do not even read the menu thoroughly before we order. We are oblivious to the entire offering of excellence and professionalism. And, we refuse to tip. We are like a civilization of Star Trek Klingons to the restaurant world. Sadly, with our inappropriate behavior, by the end of the meal, we appear to be the second-class citizens Jim Crow America said we were--when we fought so hard to prove otherwise.

The ugly truth of the matter is: if you are a black person, no one wants to serve you. No...seriously. No one wants to serve black folks, even other black folks. Servers run the other way when they see black folks coming, even other black servers. It does not matter what type of black person you are when you walk into the establishment—all that matters is that you are black. You may look nice and be well-dressed. You may be well-spoken and friendly. You may even be well-known and famous. However, more often than not, your server has been shorted and abused so many times by others who look just like you, that the server simply refuses to serve your kind. Period.

"Oh Shit, Here They Come."

I have heard this exact statement so many times, from the mouths of servers of all races in varied restaurants all over the city of Atlanta. The driving force of this book is the fact that this statement is particularly reserved only for black people. I define it as such,

> *OS-HTC: /ō SHIT hir thā kəm/, noun. – verbal phrase; exclamatory in nature, regularly declared by undertipped restaurant staff, symbolizing an emotionally overwhelming gut feeling of anxiety, accompanied by a physical facial expression of sincere disappointment and an audible exhale from the throat, compelled by a deep psychological wish*

> *that the colored folks at the host stand will not be seated in their section*

People in the restaurant industry have even trained themselves to know when big groups of black folks are coming. African-Americans put on huge productions of so many varieties, especially in the city of Atlanta. Hair shows, awards shows, car and bike shows and music festivals are held at certain times throughout the year. Droves of black people travel from all over the country to attend these events. Servers know when massive black events are headed to the city, and some avoid working during those times. Additionally, some servers avoid working on Sunday afternoons because black folks tend to congregate at restaurants after church service. Not many people have the emotional and the mental capacities to deal with so many black people at once like this. It's just too much disrespect, belligerence and penny-pinching in one place at one time.

Servers are suffering, having psychological anxiety from having to deal with black folks. The internet is inundated with blogposts and videos from disgruntled, teary-eyed servers, discombobulated over why black people behave in such ways. When it comes to serving black folks, black servers, who perhaps generally love all things black, are having to struggle with feelings of internal racism. *Why do I feel this way about my own people? Am I a hypocrite?* And the poor white servers, some of the nicest people in the world, have no idea what to do with their anxiety from black guests. They, too, are forced to reassess their beliefs about black people from these direct experiences with us. *Why do I feel this way about those people? Am I a racist?* Poor servers go through so much drama with black folks so much, they prefer not to deal with us at all, and they avoid us at all costs.

It has never been easy to discuss or handle issues of race in America; however, race always pops up everywhere in America as an issue. The problem is, in this case, everyone is afraid to talk about it. "The issue of how African Americans tip is so filled with tension, fear, anger and ignorance that waiters and restaurant owners will only whisper about it among themselves in hushed, embarrassed tones," (Dublanica, 2010). Dublanica, too, has witnessed firsthand the sneaky, secret whisperings among restaurant staff about what happened at "the black table." Servers are in the back, distraught with grief and desperation about the drama at "the black table." Servers are often in the kitchen asking co-workers to drop things off at "the black table" because they refuse to walk back by that table again. Servers send each other by "the black table" to get a good look at who's seated there. This way they recognize you when you return and warn others that you are there. The most popular subject in the kitchen is usually what happened at "the black table." As Steve Dublanica so adequately sums up in *Keep the Change*, the entire issue revolving around the way black folks tip is "one of the industry's dirty little secrets," (2010).

Nevertheless, talking about it is most crucial to understanding the dilemma. However, we must bring this conversation out from the back of the restaurant kitchen and into the dining room, so to speak. We must have this racial dialogue openly. When we sit down together and have the discussion to clear the misunderstanding, there is no need for war. Rather than whispering about race behind the door, it is time to turn up the volume on this particular issue of race in America and confront our collective fears head on—together.

This phenomenon—black folks don't tip—is not just merely rumor among the service industry underground. In his 2003 study of cultural tipping practices, "Ethnic Differences in Tipping," Dr. Michael Lynn found that black folks do indeed tip less than whites, (Dublanica, 2010). It "isn't urban legend or a racist stereotype, but a mathematically quantifiable reality," (Dublanica, 2010). In his research, Dr. Lynn discovered that blacks were less knowledgeable about tipping standards. He concluded that lower incomes and less education were factors in the tipping disparity between the two races. However, throughout all his research, Dr. Lynn still did not find a conclusive explanation as to why successful black folks refused to tip according to societal norms. Even when we are educated and rich, we still do not tip properly. Why not? Until now, understanding this phenomenon has been a puzzling mystery.

There is a small population among black folks who are proper tippers. There is an even smaller population of black folks who are very generous tippers. Perhaps some people simply enjoy giving. However, my research confirms that black folks who dare tip over 20 percent usually overtip—on purpose. Most of these overtippers have some connection, whether direct or indirect, to the service industry. Either they are currently working as tipped employees in the service industry, or, perhaps they were servers or bartenders in a past life. Or, they have a loved one who works or has worked in the past as a tipped employee, and they personally understand the server struggle. Either they've heard the outrageous stories, or they know firsthand from experience what it feels like to be in the tipped employee position. Whatever the case, they overtip to intentionally separate themselves from the tipping bunch.

This group of people, the overtippers, understand there is a disconnection between the way we tip and the way we *should* tip.

They overtip because they *know* that black folks don't tip. They feel responsible for those who don't tip and feel obligated to make up the difference. They want to set the example and be the exception to the Negro Tip Phenomenon (Chapter 1). They want to break the cycle. They consciously understand that overtipping helps balance out the universal prejudice taking place at the tables. Overtipping helps to remove the tipping stigma and reverse the negative stereotyping of black folks. Ultimately, it appears that the first lessons on proper tipping are being taught by those hailing from the service industry—those tipped employees, and the people who love them, who dine out and choose to do unto others as they would have others do to themselves.

Sadly, because of the way some of us choose to behave when we dine out, black people have become the shame and embarrassment of American dining culture. Black folks have been accused of depreciating the value of nice places. The mere presence of black folks has been the blame for creating economic disparity and lowering revenues for otherwise profitable businesses. This includes our own black-owned restaurants in our own black communities. Unknowingly, we are shortchanging ourselves by leaving an impressive negative mark upon the African-American race. We are offering justification to the negative remarks that others make about us as well as the negative stereotypes we refuse to believe about ourselves. If no one wants to serve black folks, then this means that African-Americans are being profiled from the moment we walk through the restaurant door, any restaurant door. The fact that this is true is a monumental marvel. We must hold ourselves accountable for the roles we play in this social production. We owe ourselves the dignity to correct our awful part in this, to redefine who we are, to ourselves, and to the rest of the world.

1

THE NEGRO TIP PHENOMENON

The only gift I have to give, is the ability to receive.
If giving is a gift, and it surely is, then my gift to you is to allow you to give to me.
—Jarod Kintz

Definition

The Negro Tip Phenomenon is a psychological pattern whereby a black person dines out and expects poor service because he or she is black, while simultaneously, the waitperson expects that because the guest is black, he or she may not leave a proper tip.

Explanation

The black person is hopeful for great service but is apprehensive about receiving it—so accustomed to racial discrimination. The server is hopeful that the black person will be respectful and will tip them properly. However, the server is so familiar with abuse from the black guest, he or she approaches the table already full of fear.

Based on the *last* bad dining experience, black guests enter the *next* dining experience with service anxiety. Automatically, they go into the restaurant on edge and with their guards up high. As much as they want to have a wonderful experience this time, they are reminiscent of the bad experience from last time. Instead of focusing on having a great time today, they are dreading a repeat of the dining encounter from yesterday. Within the attempt for understanding, they inevitably begin to question if racism is involved, "Maybe it was because I am black that I received such poor service. Will it happen again this time?" Now, they are bracing themselves for racism. Meaning, they are arming themselves and preparing for table battle. If they must endure a punch, they will return every blow. They are ready to catch every sarcastic remark or flippant statement from a potentially racially motivated server, and they quickly reply with a highly intelligent or equally ghetto snap back. And, at this point, they are inherently on guard for any neglect in service and flaws with the food. And even more, they are so tired of receiving continuous racially motivated inferior service that they just may use the dining opportunity to aggravate the hell of the server, create chaos in the restaurant and not leave a tip. The guests do not do this simply because it makes them feel better. They are playing psychology against economics to win a socio-ethical restaurant war.

Imagine the scenario. The server approaches. Before a single word is exchanged, there is already fear and anxiety reeking from the table of black folks, and there is fear and anxiety in the approaching server. Everybody is on guard and filled with tension, drawing on the expectation of a bad experience. But why is the server afraid, anxious? The server, too, is drawing from his last experience with the last set of black folks he served. He is not prepared to deliver his best service. As much as he wants to offer a wonderful experience this time, he is reminiscent of the bad experience from last time. Instead of focusing on having a great time today, he is dreading a repeat of the dining encounter from yesterday. Within the attempt for understanding, he inevitably begins to question with racism involved, "Maybe it is because they are black that they sabotage good service, that they don't tip. Will it happen again this time?" Now, he is bracing himself for disrespect. The server is ready to catch every sarcastic remark or flippant statement from a potentially abusive guest and quickly braces himself for unnecessary displays of high intelligence or equally ghetto snap backs. And, at this point, he is automatically prepared for the guest to find even the slightest faults in service and bullshit flaws with the food. And even more, he is so tired of the continuously disrespectful behavior that he just may use the abuse as an excuse to perform a half-assed job. From his perspective, he probably will not get tipped for his hard work, anyway. He may leave the party waiting much longer than normal and not mention the restaurant specials. He may not return to the table to check on them nor refill their beverages. He will take his time to get their food to the table and leave them panting for the check. After all, it's psychological warfare.

Self-Fulfilling Prophecy

This example is simply a situation of self-fulfilling prophecy, occurring from both sides of the dining spectrum. Servers continue to expect the worst treatment from black dining patrons, and black folks at the table continue to expect the worst service. Everyone acts according to his or her own expectations, and everybody gets exactly what they expect. The black folks get poor service; the server gets a poor tip or no tip at all. Interestingly, both parties end up confused, wondering what happened. Black folks question why they always end up with bad service, as the server wonders why it is that black folks never leave a good tip. The two queries are intricately interwoven. Lynn & Brewster of the Washington Post (2015) agree that the way black folks tip "has been linked to the delivery of relatively inferior service to black customers." Citing a national survey of restaurant servers, the Washington Post article reports that "over half of the respondents admitted that they don't always give their best effort when waiting on black customers," (Lynn & Brewster, 2015).

It is apparent that the two parties are in this dilemma are equally yoked, matched with one's expectations of the other. Accordingly, and as expected, as by whatever means of law of attraction, the quality of service is ultimately poor, resulting in, of course, a poor tip or no tip at all.

From these expectations, the worst scenario takes place between the two—every single time. Before either knows it, each party is participating in this duel on both conscious and subconscious levels. The dominating fear embedded within the exchange can take an energy all its own and escalate the situation far beyond the control of either party involved.

All day, every day—breakfast, lunch and dinner—from city to city across the nation, this racially-charged psychological ritual is taking place at the American restaurant table. It makes a massive statement about race relations in America. It offers a great deal of information regarding our current prejudices as a nation. We simply do not trust each other to do the right thing, and it is shaping the future of our race relations. If this problem is occurring daily, from restaurant to restaurant, then the dining experience can also be a great platform for change, for racial tolerance and for a re-assessment of our prejudices toward each other. When does it end? Where is the happy medium for both the diner and the server?

Servers, just like those in any other profession, do not desire to be abused, disregarded and disrespected. They usually choose serving because they actually *like* people. It's their job to be nice. When it comes to serving black people, however, they are apprehensive and afraid. They fear an exchange with black restaurant guests will be one wrought with confusion and emptiness, that they will be overworked and underpaid.

Black people enjoy dining out just like everyone else. They fear, though, that when they go out to eat, they will receive poor service, simply because they are black. Among themselves, black people know this as almost certain truth. All black folks have experienced some form of racial discrimination while dining out. Of course, racism is not specific to the restaurant arena. Black people experience racial discrimination in all forms of life--work, school, organization, competition, and dining too. There is no denying this. Discrimination is so rampant in everyday black life that it's like polluted air black folks are forced to breathe. Racial discrimination is expected. Black folks know it's coming, so black folks brace themselves for it. Although black folks are forced to deal with racial discrimination, they won't voluntarily pay anyone money for it. So being, on the restaurant battleground, not tipping is a powerful weapon.

Herein lies the true dilemma. There are times in the dining environment when racial discrimination does not occur. However, this does not change the outcome. The end result remains the same. In the absence of any discrimination at all, and in the presence of immaculate service, black folks *still* do not tip properly. In the absence of poverty, and with the presence of high levels of income, black folks *still* do not tip properly. When black folks walk into the restaurant environment with preconceived negative notions about the outcome, they set themselves up for failure. Without the education and the understanding of what is required at the table, a horrible experience is inevitable. Additionally, when black people do not behave properly, they help sabotage an otherwise beautiful dining experience. Often without even realizing it, black people contribute significantly to the very poor circumstances they experience when dining.

Middle ground between these two forces can be found somewhere between knowledge and understanding. Ignorant behavior must be replaced by knowledge. Diners must be knowledgeable of what is required in a fine dining experience in order to enjoy a nice meal in public. Servers must understand the diversity of the guests whom they serve and be able to maintain great service, even as they adjust to the complexities of the situation and the tension between the races. Though the issue is huge, it can be resolved simply with a little mutual respect, patience, consideration and empathy.

KASSONDRA ROCKSWELL

The fighting continues, but no one wins a war.

2

BLACK FOLKS DON'T BEHAVE

Exploring Disposition

Temperament & Tendencies in Uncharted Territory

Rudeness is merely the expression of fear. People fear they won't get what they want.
The most dreadful and unattractive person only needs to be loved...
and they will open up like a flower.
—"The Grand Budapest Hotel" by Wes Anderson, 2014

The way black folks behave in a restaurant is just as important as the way they pay the bill. Many times, the attitude and behavior exhibited by black people in this setting are the very factors that sabotage the dining experience. Some of this behavior happens unknowingly. Other times, it happens with malice and intention. Nevertheless, it does happen, and it affects the entire experience. Disposition is about mentality, character and temperament. The way black folks think, speak and act is crucial at the table. Poor table disposition sets a negative tone for the dinner and makes it extremely difficult for excellent service to take place.

Attitude

Many times, negative restaurant behavior is already in place before black people take a seat. They walk into the restaurant already disgruntled and pessimistic towards the experience. When the friendly server approaches the table in an attempt to satisfy the requests of the guests, they start the exchange with disinterest and a discourteous attitude. The scene is reminiscent of a teacher standing before a classroom of new students on the first day of school and every child is afraid to raise his hand and speak up. They refuse to return the greeting. They refuse to smile. They are apathetic towards the server's suggestions. They are completely unwilling to accept kindness and hesitant to show any form of gratitude. This hesitance to be cordial—this abandonment of kindness—creates a cloud of awkward confusion that hovers over the table during the entire meal. What can come of this except disaster?

Why does this attitude exist? Do black people simply walk around angry all the time? Are black people just generally unhappy everywhere they go? Were these folks arguing in the car during the ride to the restaurant? What is this obvious discomfort? From where does it come?

It all starts at the restaurant. This is a thing—a phenomenon. Some folks are just assholes. They exist in every race, every color. They will make any situation uncomfortable. They have no idea how to or when to requests things. However, they are the exception here. If the asshole character type is removed from this equation, the remainder of the people are nice, decent folks. So why are nice, decent folks sitting at the table with such attitude? The same happy couple, the same jovial group of people who were engaged in conversation and laughter just moments before entering a restaurant will, once at the table, become stoic, reserved and dispirited. Why is this so?

Well, for black folks, in the restaurant arena there are many psychological dynamics at play. The overwhelming uneasiness can be attributed to several factors. One or more of the following issues is taking place.

They are bracing for racism.

Black people know racism very well. They are so familiar with discrimination that they can sense it. They can feel it coming. They know when they are being profiled or targeted. They know when others feel uncomfortable with their presence. When they sit down to dine, they are gauging the situation. A one-on-one human interaction is about to take place, and they are readying themselves for race to be its most significant factor. They are determining whether or not the server is discomforted by them. They are bracing themselves for disrespect. They are waiting to see how they will be treated. Although these feelings are understandable, they stiffen the personalities at the table. With everyone on edge, the nice, decent black folks simply appear to be tight-lipped and rude.

They are afraid of the bill.

Often times when a party is behaving with a high level of insecurity, it is because they have come to the restaurant with mixed emotions about spending so much money on a meal. Apparently, they hadn't even thought about the prices of the meal until they actually saw them on the menu. The expensive prices are startling, which takes them aback a bit. It is highly likely that the entire party is experiencing a form of collective anxiety over the anticipated amount of the bill. They are unable to relax and enjoy the experience because they are fretting over how much the meal is going to cost. Without paper or pen, they are performing mathematical computations in their heads to see how this one meal is going to affect their bank balance. They should be enjoying dinner, but they are thinking about gas money and bills. They order the food, and they attempt to go with the flow. Meanwhile, they are having second thoughts about how much they are spending. Inevitably, being there (and spending so much) feels foolish.

This anxiety is often mistaken as indifference or lack of interest. However, it is fear—plain and simple. Black folks have the money, but they are afraid to spend it. It takes a great deal of composure to recuperate from the realization that one is sacrificing the electric bill for an overpriced meal. And this realization puts a great deal of pressure on the experience. The guest feels that if they spend so much on the meal, the entire experience had better be absolutely flawless. The food had better be the best they've ever had, and the server had better not make a single mistake.

They are new to the experience.

Only 50 years or so have passed since the American civil rights movement prompted changes in social equality. Barely 60 years have passed since black people fought for desegregation—the right to dine in the same room as white guests. It was only a couple of generations ago that segregation was made illegal by law. The entire notion of black folks dining in fine restaurants is a relatively recent one. Many black people have never visited a fancy restaurant, so there are many who are still visiting fine dining restaurants for the first time. It's like stepping into the unknown. The elaborate décor and the luxurious ambiance may be quite a contrast to what they are accustomed to. The menu is full of unrecognizable European words. The table may be pre-set with three different forks and three different glasses, and they don't know which one to use. The experience can be intimidating. So yes, black guests may be uncomfortable, which is natural and understandable. However, this discomfort can be mistaken for apathy. To the server, it feels like they just don't want to be there.

They are putting on airs.

People handle table insecurity in different ways. Some choose the game of pretend. They are unfamiliar with the atmosphere and try to hide it by faking over-familiarity. They act as if they have been frequenting nice restaurants for years. They pretend to be comfortable, and it is obvious they are pretending by their exaggerated behavior. They are arrogant, snooty and pretentious. Then they proceed to mispronounce menu items and grape varietals. Or, they have no idea what temperature to choose when they order a steak. The problem here is that they are behaving the way they *think* rich people behave, so for them it is okay to be snappy and demanding towards the server. This, too, complicates the dining experience. While the guest is pretending to know everything, he is missing out on learning things that might guarantee a great experience. It is obvious to the server that the guest is pretending, and it is difficult to deliver excellent service while dancing around this pretense.

On rare occasion, a party of black people will admit to their server that they are new to the restaurant—that they are clueless about what to order. They cordially ask for help with the menu, and they are unembarrassed about seeking assistance on how to order properly. This method of questioning is ideal, as it is honest and respectable. It is more sensible than pretending to know what they are doing, when it is obvious they are clueless about how to proceed. Plus, by opening themselves to learn something new, they set themselves up for an evening of anticipation and excitement.

Indecision

It starts from the moment black folks walk in. They have no idea where they would like to be seated. The restaurant host will walk black people to a wonderful table. They don't want to sit there. The host will direct them to a different table. They don't want to sit there. Other times, the server will greet the table and take everyone's drink orders. By the time the server returns with their drinks, they are gone. The table is empty. They preferred to sit somewhere else, so they got up and moved without warning, without informing anyone. There is nothing wrong with requesting a different table, but black people will often move two or three times, to two or three different sections, before they discover that Goldilocks feeling—a seat that feels "just right." And this is if they decide to stay at all. Sometimes the server will return with the drinks only to discover they've completely left the building. They changed their minds and decided to eat somewhere else, so they got up and left without warning. Sometimes black people sit down and plan on eating, but once the menu arrives, the prices scare them away. With the stealth of a super-intelligent entity, they disappear without a trace. When moving to another table or leaving the restaurant, it is appropriate to inform the staff, so they can manage the situation and adjust to an unexpected departure. To leave without a word is tacky and rude. Such cowardly behavior is both inconsiderate and immature.

For those who do decide to stay at the restaurant—given they have found satisfactory seating—they have no idea what they want to order. They don't read the menu, not really. They don't know what cocktail to choose. They want wine but have no clue what kind. They can't even decide between sweet tea and lemonade. Then, when they finally order something to drink, they drink half of it, then send it back because they didn't like it.

It's the same thing with the food. No one reads the menu, not really. They refuse to decide. Many times, black guests will not choose an entrée until they see what others at the table are going to eat first. Servers have to painstakingly explain every detail about each entrée and answer a million questions to help them make a decision. When they finally order something, soon after they change it to something else. The server goes to ring in the order. Then 10 minutes later, they are flagging the server down to change the order again.

Why wait until everyone else has ordered before making a decision? Many times, this indecision is based on money. This is another example of how economics is a crucial factor in black folks' exceptional table behavior. They want to know how much the other person is spending. Subsequently, they make their decision based on how much an entrée costs rather than choosing the food they truly desired. Dissatisfaction is inevitable.

Then, other times, they simply refuse to be outdone. It is as if they want to make sure no one else at the table "out-orders" them, like ordering is some type of competition. For example, a table of older black ladies were ordering po' boy sandwiches for lunch one day. The second lady asked for the bread on her po' boy sandwich to be "extra crispy." After the order was placed, the server was summoned back to the table. Suddenly, all the other ladies now wanted extra crispy bread too. The server goes back to the kitchen to explain to the frustrated cook that the whole table wants extra crispy bread. The ladies receive their food, and one of them calls the server over again. "How come her shrimp bigger than mine?" she asks. She wants her sandwich returned to the kitchen and replaced with bigger shrimp.

This request has upset an otherwise smooth lunch experience because now one lady must sit for several minutes with no meal while everyone else enjoys their food. By the time her bigger shrimp arrive, the other ladies are halfway through their meals. Then, when it was time to clear the used dishes from the table, it was evident that not one of these women had even touched the extra crispy bread. They merely ate the shrimp and oysters that were inside the bread. All that perfectly extra crispy bread went straight to the garbage. In refusing to be outdone, the ladies lost the ability to think for themselves, adding unnecessary complications to what could have been a drama-free lunch.

Because of the constant indecision, the server has to spend so much more time at black folks' tables, attempting to cater to their every need amidst continuous confusion. Not only do the constant changes interrupt the flow of that one table, they affect the quality of service to all of that server's other tables as well. If it's bad enough, indecision can even disrupt the flow of food in the kitchen, affecting the service in the entire restaurant.

Distrust

Black people in general are not very trusting of anything of a governmental, institutional or corporate structure. Large companies and big businesses are symbols of capitalism, and capitalism has been the driving force of injustice among black people. Having been historically abused, systematically violated and secretly experimented on, black folks are somewhat suspicious of these entities—restaurants included. Of course, black people *choose* to go out. They decide for themselves to go out for dinner, but they do not necessarily trust the establishment. They do not trust the place to be clean. They do not trust the food will be prepared to their liking. They do not trust that the receipt will be correct. Still, they attempt the journey nonetheless, in search of a great time.

Because black people have a strong history of working in the back of house, they know what goes on back there. As chaotic as it can be in the back, many things slip through the cracks, including cleanliness. So, when a black guest asks for plasticware, it is most likely because she does not trust the silverware is clean. As well, when a black guest asks for a cup of hot water and proceeds to soak her silverware in it, it is because she does not trust the restaurant to provide clean utensils. Uncertain of what goes on in the kitchen, she may feel justified in her actions, but it does not make her look any less silly. Black folks are the only people who commit this horrible etiquette crime. They do this unapologetically, without hesitation and with no shame. They request the hot water and after soaking the silverware for several minutes, they sit there and clean it with a napkin right at the table in front of everyone. It is the tackiest, most absurd, mind-baffling thing anyone could ever witness.

It is rather ridiculous to choose to eat at a place, then, at the same time, shamelessly convey that one does not trust the place to be clean. Why eat there at all? Ironically, if the silverware is not clean, then the cup the silverware sits inside may not be clean either. If one does not trust that the silverware is clean, then why trust the plates or glasses or any of the dishes to be clean? Using the restaurant silverware is not the only way of contracting germs from the establishment. If the restaurant does not take the time to disinfect and polish the silverware, then the silverware would be the smallest of concerns. There would undoubtedly be a lack of cleanliness in dozens of other inconspicuous places (detailed in Chapter 5). There is simply no place for such a foolish gesture as soaking your fork amidst the dining population of intelligent people. Essentially, black folks who do this are dining in a place they do not trust, but oddly with the expectation of a pleasant experience. This way of thinking is a tad bit illogical.

Some black people do not trust that the delightfully friendly server is genuine. The nicer the server is to them, the more aggravated they become. They believe the server is only pretending to be nice in order to get a good tip. So instead of returning the courtesy, they become precautious and guarded, warding off any notions of sincerity, as if to say, "Please don't be extra nice to me, you're not getting an extra tip."

Most black people would like to have a good time, but they don't necessarily trust anybody else to deliver it. In effect, they take control of the dining situation, believing they must dictate every segment of the experience in order for things to turn out great. The entire point of visiting a nice restaurant is to be able to sit back, relax and enjoy the experience. This requires putting one's happiness in the hands of another. It means trusting the staff to do its job, allowing the restaurant to offer its excellence and trusting the flow of everything to bring pleasure and joy. This cannot happen if the guest is constantly interrupting and redirecting and manipulating the experience. If black folks would approach the experience from a more trusting perspective, they might realize dining pleasures beyond their expectations.

Exceptions, Substitutions, Modifications and Extras

The chef is the MVP in a fine dining restaurant. Because of their crucial role in selecting the food and creating the menu, chefs carry a great deal of power in this arena. They are the ones who choose every single ingredient in every dish—from the meat and potatoes all the way to the salt and pepper. They have painstakingly slaved over these culinary creations to ensure a harmony among the ingredients which will stimulate all the human senses. Each ingredient balances the flavor, which radiates subtly throughout the dish. It's not just steak, chicken and fish to them. Their job is to elevate steak, chicken and fish to new levels. They prefer that you enjoy the meal exactly the way it is prepared. When people ask them to make changes to their food, it's destructive to their creation. It is insulting to the chef and insulting to the restaurant to disregard the food in this way. It sabotages the dining experience. To chefs, it is complete disrespect for the dish. And it pisses them off. Because of this, chefs do not take kindly to guests requesting modifications to their dishes.

Even in this hyper-allergy age, when everyone seems to be allergic to something, chefs hold firm to the "no modifications" rule. They may make small exceptions if feasible, like a request for "no nuts." For the most part, however, no one is special enough for a culinary pardon. In an article on Chow.com, Helena Echlin (2011) confirms that some upscale restaurants refuse to omit ingredients from the dish, while others refuse to make any exceptions to the dish at all. This is regardless of pregnancy, allergy or celebrity. Instead, patrons with allergies must choose from whatever allergen-free dishes are available on the menu. If a guest is allergic to nuts, dairy, gluten, shellfish or any other food, he should check out the menu well-beforehand and have an idea what is available to him at that restaurant. This holds true for vegetarians and vegans as well and any others with special dietary needs. Chefs can be very strict about their modification policies.

Most people do enjoy the chef's dish, as is. Black people, however, seem to look at the way an entrée is prepared as merely a suggestion. They seem to come to the table with an alternative preparation already in mind. They have no qualms about requesting extensive exceptions and modifications to their meals. These requests are so frequent and so odd among black folks that dissatisfaction appears to be a racial character trait. They do not understand (or, perhaps, they do not care) that the dish was meticulously envisioned, fussed over, made and remade until it was perfect. Black folks request so many changes to a meal, the food is not even recognizable as a menu item anymore.

- Spinach salad made with no spinach, romaine lettuce instead, substitute cucumbers with tomatoes, substitute cheddar for feta, add croutons, no nuts, extra dressing
- Steak that's been marinated in seasonings for 48 hours, but with no marinated seasoning
- Grilled chicken that is only available grilled, fried

Of course, the chef has all the ingredients to fry chicken, and surely he knows *how* to fry chicken, but fried chicken is nowhere on the restaurant's menu. Many black patrons want to make unfamiliar recipes familiar, trying to force familiarity into the meal. They never step out of their boxes to try something new. The restaurant is not prepared to make meals for them the way their moms make them at home. It is best to keep exceptional requests to a minimum and be open to try something new.

Then, there are the requests for extras. Extra sauce. Extra bread. Extra crispy. Extra butter. Extra lemons. Extra ketchup. Extra seasoning. Extra dressing. Extra ice. Ice on the side. Extra well done. Extra to go boxes. It's just too much.

Small requests can become overwhelming when everyone at the table needs two or three little modifications and two or three extra things. Even worse, these same black folks often have the nerve to become impatient. Until now, black people have not realized what it takes to acquire all these extras and make all these modifications happen. All the requests for modifications and extras take an extraordinary amount of time and energy. They have to be meticulously entered into the computer system in whatever method the restaurant requires, which can take several minutes. Then, the server has to go to the kitchen and explain all these modifications to the kitchen, which also can take several minutes—even longer if the server has to respectfully wait until the chef stops yelling at them for making his already complicated job more complicated. Unbeknownst to the guest, the server may have to travel down three flights of stairs and back, perhaps to an outside cooler or storage area, just to retrieve an "extra" item for them. Meanwhile, the table of black folks who requested all the changes wonder what's taking so long, while the service to the server's other tables is cast into jeopardy. Then, it is quite possible and highly likely that someone at the table of black folks who requested all the changes will ultimately be dissatisfied with something and send it back to the kitchen. It's just way too much.

Black folks request all these items, only to leave them on the table unused and untouched. It is as if they needed them for comfort, to feel as if they had more than enough, to help balance the feeling of lack, of not having enough at all. Seemingly, they request the extra items to counter this emotion. So, they ask for unnecessary, extra stuff, just in case, then they never use it. They become extraordinarily wasteful in this regard.

As mentioned in the previous section, *Distrust*, there are issues of trust here. Perhaps the meal will taste okay, but they are not willing to take the chance on it. If they must spend so much money on a meal, it had better be good. When money is at stake, it forces them to choose what they are used to, what they can count on. So, they modify the meal to make it more identifiable, more trustworthy. Who wants to spend a whole lot of money on something they really didn't like that much? Not black folks. The only way to ensure the food is good to them is to modify it to their personal, particular liking and surround themselves with extra items.

These extensive requests are attempts for control. Just like trying to control the seating (as mentioned in the earlier section *Indecision*), they are trying to control the food and the entire experience. That way, the money sacrificed for all of it can be justified. It is simply a psychological attempt to justify the money spent. It is as if to say, "If I'm going to spend all this money, I want everything to be exactly the way I want it." This behavior is apparent at tables of black people from all different financial backgrounds. It is deeply embedded in the psychological mentality of the people. Most black people grapple with ideals about money and spending, no matter how much money they have.

Despite the fact that exceptions are simply annoying as hell, there are many sensible reasons why a restaurant would refuse to make modifications and substitutions. First of all, for example, if you take a salad from the menu, remove the olives, add cheese to it and then change the dressing, the chef cannot guarantee that it will taste great. No one has tested this oliveless salad with cheese and a different dressing. If the guest does not enjoy it, there is now room for criticism and disappointment, and even the threat of a disgruntled visit to the friendly internet review forum to bash the restaurant. Echlin, who runs a *Table Manners* blog, mentions in her article, *When Restaurants Refuse Substitutions* (2011), that quality control is one driving force in requiring guests to stick to the menu. Modifications and substitutions have grown so out of control that many upscale restaurants are now printing the refusal policy on their menus. One restaurant Los Angeles restaurant, *Gjelina,* kindly states:

> *Changes & Modifications politely declined.* (Echlin, 2011)

Zambri's, a restaurant in Victoria, British Columbia, is more specific:

> *Substitutions politely declined. While modifications & substitutions may seem easy to accommodate, these requests compromise the unique characteristics of our food & the efficiency of our service.* (The Primalist, 2012).

Among those restaurants that have not yet banned substitutions, many still charge their patrons a fee for any substitutions to their dishes. In light of fine dining restaurants adopting this new policy, it is clear that too many exceptions are a nuisance to the experience. This has become such a problem, that offering a flat-out "no" to the customer is trending among restaurants, dismissing the old service adage that "the customer is always right." It is statistically difficult to assess how much black folks' behavior has contributed to the new trend of restaurants refusing to modify their dishes. However, it is quite possible some restaurants have instituted such policies to specifically deter black clientele from these practices or perhaps steer them away from their businesses altogether. Clearly, the dire requests for exceptions and modifications are too much for restaurants to handle.

Life is about the currency between people. Humans grow most, not by sitting at home, withdrawn and alone, but from their interaction with others. Fine restaurants are primed and ready to cultivate this type of exchange, but it must be allowed to take place. It is not necessarily about how to get exactly what's wanted as much as it is about going with flow and allowing what's wanted to naturally manifest. It is about engaging the moment and creating a memorable life experience. This cannot happen for black people if they venture into the world yet refuse to positively interact with others and appreciate the value of what others in the world have to offer. There is so much more to be gained if they learn to see beyond themselves and allow others to help facilitate a joyful, unforgettable experience.

Self-Importance

As mentioned earlier in this chapter, some black people start their dining experience by "putting on airs." This happens as a result of being insecure in a new environment. Some others, however, seem to be just insecure in life in general. They need everyone to know they are important. They carry a sense of self-urgency everywhere they go. They want special treatment and unwarranted recognition constantly. When these people dine out, their propensity for neediness becomes highly unreasonable and unapologetically overbearing. They are attempting to mask these insecurities with an air of self-righteousness and self-entitlement. It is a role they play in order to appear knowledgeable and in control, when in reality they are dealing with issues of worthiness. It is obvious they are trying to prove they belong.

They ask for the "other" menu, when there is no other menu available. They want the server to sing them the happy birthday song, when the restaurant does not offer that service. They want their steak to look as big as everyone else's steak, or they will send it back, even though the filets weigh the same. They order things they cannot pronounce, while pretending to know how to pronounce it. It is not so much that they want to look smart as much as it is that they do not want to appear stupid. There is a difference. If they were truly smart, they would know it is normal to encounter unrecognized language on a food menu. What is not smart, however, is pretending to know how to pronounce a word, then screwing it up. It makes more sense to simply ask the server for the correct pronunciation of the word, and learn something new. Rather than learn a new word to add to their dining language repertoire, many black folks go home, having enjoyed food and wine that they still cannot pronounce correctly. Apparently, pretense is more important than actual knowledge.

Feigning self-importance leads to lying, and self-important black folks often play make-believe to get their way. For instance, they will complain that the soup is too salty, just so it can be remade for them. So self-concerned, they don't realize that the soup was made as a big batch in a big pot that other guests have been enjoying all evening with no complaints. A self-important guest will send the same flawless meal back three times. They need extra attention. If the food is truly unenjoyable, a sensible person would simply choose another entrée, order something else from the menu. But a self-important guest? No way. These folks require undivided attention. Rather than order something different, they will have the same meal sent back and forth to the kitchen and have it remade over and over. It's never about the food. It's all for show. This guest must make it clear to everyone that they are self-proclaimed VIP of the table, and they will do this by any means necessary. They disregard the feelings of everyone else around them. They make everyone uncomfortable. When they do this, they embarrass the others in their party and disrupt the flow of service. While everyone else is finished eating their food, the self-important person is still complaining about their meal, making a scene. They need another remake, or they want the meal for free, or they want to speak with the manager—whatever it takes to maintain themselves as the center of attention.

The most interesting display of self-importance shows up in the form of poorly planned birthday dinners, whereby black folks reserve large tables and private rooms for themselves...and no one shows up. Many times, young black folks book reservations for large parties, to celebrate with 15 to 20 people. The problem is, only six or seven people may actually show up. And the folks who do make it to the party, show up late. And out of those six or seven who show up late, maybe two or three will actually order something to eat.

Envision the scenario. A table, set with 20 seats for 20 guests. The birthday girl—the first to arrive at her own party—has been sitting alone for at least half an hour, waiting on her buddies to show up. They trickle in tardy for the party, perhaps one or two at a time. Eventually, only eight or so people end up scattered around 12 empty chairs. Sweating water glasses with melting ice cubes sit next to lonely, unused menus in front of seats with no people in them. The guest of honor came prepared to order whatever she wanted. After all, it's her birthday. She has a cocktail, an appetizer and an entrée. However, her friend sitting next to her is sipping water and still picking at the free bread the server dropped off before she even got there. A couple of the other friends order no food at all but are nursing free refills of sweet tea. No one is really eating, except the birthday girl. No one is prepared to spend any money in honor of the celebration. No joke is being told. No one is leading a funny story to share amongst the group. There is no laughter, no fun. Each of them is just sitting there, like they don't even know each other, like they don't care to get to know each other at all. They have chosen to celebrate at a place which focuses on eating and drinking but hardly anyone is eating or drinking anything. Nothing celebratory is happening.

Eating and drinking have always been the foundation of celebration. Eating creates conversation about the food that leads to further conversation. Dining together promotes sharing and invokes laughter—necessary for a good time. Drinking wets the palate and soothes the mind, allowing each person to break her own ice, let her hair down and be open for a natural exchange in conversation. Without the food and drink, the party is set for failure. Without the laughter, the party is doomed. No celebration is likely to occur.

In essence, the guest of honor planned a party for herself and only a few people showed up. They showed up late. They did not eat. They brought no gifts. None of them even offered to pay for her bill or a portion thereof. They made no preparations or sacrifice to ensure a celebration in her honor. The birthday lady may have had a more successful celebration by planning something for a few friends, or even just for herself. On the contrary, she planned to entertain a party of 20 and was met with disappointment. Either she did not plan this party well, or she has some interesting friends.

Nevertheless, the circumstance reeks of an attempt at self-importance, gone awry. In her defense, she is not alone in this predicament. Black folks, especially black women, do this all the time. They make reservations for large numbers and then realize a small, pathetic turnout. It brings into question whether or not black women are as important as they think they are to the people they keep in their circles. It also challenges black women's ideals of self-worth and the ways they choose to feel valuable. Issues of self-importance should perhaps be replaced with quests for the true meaning of friendship, the reevaluation of loyalty to loved ones and the understanding of what's really real.

Meanwhile, the poor server who was responsible for serving this group was prompted to serve a party of 20, which realistically ended up being a party of eight that, altogether, spent enough money to total a bill equivalent to a party of three. Amidst all the uncertainty and social dysfunction, self-important guests can become a server's worst nightmare.

HOT ASS MESS IN A HOT ORANGE DRESS

In the summer of 2014, I worked as a server in a fine dining restaurant located at the infamous Atlanta CNN Center. I had only been working there a couple of weeks when Mr. ShowTime came to town for a show at the Philips Arena (now the State Farm Arena), which is in a complex connected to the CNN Center. The restaurant was dependent upon events occurring at and around the CNN Center for its business, so we were all anticipating a dining crowd to pack the restaurant when the show was over. We were also well aware that Mr. ShowTime was coming so close to us, and everyone was hoping he would make an appearance in our store.

That weekend, perhaps the first night of the awards show festivities, I served two fine gentlemen for dinner in the restaurant dining room. They were two black men, very well-dressed, seemingly educated and cultured, accustomed to fine dining. The big guy in the nice hat was polite but mostly quiet and reserved. The gentleman with the bowtie, however, was talkative and friendly. He was quite inquisitive, and he let me know they enjoyed my service. He asked me several personal questions. He wanted to know my name, how long I had worked there, etc. He also wanted to know if I worked the following day because he said he would be back for lunch, and he wanted to ask for me by name so that I could serve him again. I guaranteed him I would be there the next day. I thought he was flirting. Regardless, I was grateful for his kindness. He was extremely nice, and he left a nice tip.

The following day during the lunch shift, in walks Mr. Bowtie. I just so happened to be standing right near the entry at the host stand when he walked into the restaurant. We kindly embraced after greeting each other by name. He then proceeded to ask the host about my section. My section consisted of four tables with four chairs each, and it was at the front of the restaurant near the tall glass windows where guests could enjoy sight-seeing pedestrians and gaze into Centennial Park across the street. Mr. Bowtie insisted on seating in a different section—a discreet section somewhere in the back of the restaurant. And, he insisted that I be his server. I was impressed with myself. I wasn't new to the game, but I was on a new team. Again, I had only been working there a couple weeks, and here was a gentleman demanding my service. I walked away to look after my tables while Mr. Bowtie discussed his seating demands with the host.

When I returned to the host stand to find out what happened with Mr. Bowtie, the host was cheesing at me with this humungous, peculiar smile. She and a couple of others started praising me black-girl-style,

> *You go girl.*
> *I see you playa.*
> *You the shit girl.*
> *Ok, go 'head then.*

I was accustomed to people requesting my service, so I was not much fazed by the episode. I laughed with them and tried to remain humble. The host then explained to me that Mr. Bowtie was bringing in a party of six, including Mr. ShowTime, and that Mr. Bowtie insisted I be the one to serve them in one of our small private dining rooms. Oh shit!

I already had four full tables. If anybody was to get a fifth table, it was not supposed to be me. There were other servers there, working with only half as much, waiting to fill their sections. Plus, the server hierarchy in that restaurant would have never allowed a newbie like me to serve someone like Mr. Showtime. There were tenured servers who had been working there for years who had seniority over me, and they were not happy. To the envy of all the veteran servers of that restaurant, I was personally requested to serve Mr. ShowTime, having only been working at that restaurant for two weeks. A little bit of ego attempted to kick in, but I decided to postpone feeling myself until after I was certain I had done a great job. After all, I already had four full tables. I wanted to give them all excellent service *and* make a lasting impression on Mr. Showtime all at the same time.

For me, serving Mr. Showtime was more than a mere opportunity to meet a celebrity. This was a spiritual encounter. I had been having a recurring dream that I was on the radio being interviewed by Mr. Showtime about this very book. For the cards to be moved around in my favor this way to ensure I would meet him, for me, was simply divine. I wanted to do my absolute best.

I made my most professional spiel of lunch features to Mr. ShowTime and his party. After I took their orders for appetizers and dropped off their drinks, something bizarre occurred. The host approached me to explain that there was "this woman" who wanted to join Mr. ShowTime's party. I reminded her that Mr. Showtime was in a small private room with five people and that the room can only hold six chairs. She told me that she had made this clear to the lady. She further explained that "this woman," along with her two friends, wanted me to ask Mr. ShowTime to move to a larger room so that they could all be seated together. I had no idea who "this woman" was. Nevertheless, my precise answer to the host was, "Hell no."

I explained to the host that I had already brought drinks to Mr. ShowTime and his party. Mr. ShowTime and his party were completely comfortable in the room which only holds six. Mr. ShowTime looked like he was extremely weary from a very long day. He'd probably been awake for days, preparing for that awards event. He was obviously exhausted. When I had dropped off his glass of Riesling, his head was laid lightly against the wall for support, and he had closed his eyes for an involuntary catnap. There was no chance in hell I was about to ask him to move. And who was "this woman" who thought she was so important that I should ask Mr. ShowTime to get up from where he was to move somewhere else, just to accommodate her? He obviously wasn't expecting her. Again, he was part of a party of six, in a private room which could only hold six people. Ask him to move? Hell to the naw. It wasn't happening. Not on my watch.

Uncertain what message the host relayed to the woman, she came back shortly after to explain that "this woman" and her two friends were now demanding to be seated in the restaurant's VIP room. Now, the VIP room was only utilized for business meetings and small private gatherings. It had one large conference-style table, immaculately set and plated for 12 people. It was a showpiece for the restaurant, and no small party was ever seated in there. Yet, the lady had demanded that her party of three be seated in that room. Because the room was not being used at the time, no server was assigned to the VIP room. And because the lady was trying to get next to Mr. Showtime, whom I was serving, the host asked me to serve them. To my own disbelief, I said okay.

I watched the hostess as she walked the party of three towards the VIP room, and I was taken aback by the woman in the front. She was a big, black woman—thick and supercurvy. She had the biggest hair in the restaurant, and it was blazing orange. Her skin-tight dress was also bright orange. She was a spectacle to behold as she sashayed across the dining room like some royal descendent of Venus Hottentot. The way the other two tagged along behind her like baby ducks gave me a chilling sensation, as I realized I was about to get into some shit. As I watched her big ass wobble down a narrow aisle towards the VIP entrance, I felt an overwhelming familiarity about her. I knew her from somewhere.

Meanwhile, I was running back and forth, all over the damn place. Mr. ShowTime's awards event that morning had just recently ended, and his guests were overflowing into the restaurant. It was busy as hell. I was trying to hold down the four tables in the front, Mr. Showtime and his private party in the back and now these three ladies in the VIP room. I entered the VIP room to meet the party of three ladies. They looked rather ridiculous and silly, the three of them sitting at a large conference table set for a party of 12. They had wasted no time destroying the table settings, having carelessly pushed aside all the plateware and glassware to make room for their purses and bags on top of the table. Now that I was up close and personal with her, I could not shake the feeling that I knew Blazing Orange from somewhere. I just could not remember from where.

Before I was able to say anything, before she asked any questions about the food or beverages, Blazing Orange made her intentions clear. She wanted to pay the bill for Mr. ShowTime's party. She asked me to fetch Mr. ShowTime's assistant, so I went to Mr. Showtime's private room to get his assistant and explained the situation. Then I walked the impressive gentleman, Mr. Capable Assistant, to the VIP room and introduced him to Blazing Orange who was demanding to pay for Mr. Showtime's bill. She insisted. Mr. Capable Assistant politely but adamantly refused. Blazing Orange starkly replied, "Please tell him that (name omitted) said hello and that I insist on taking care of his bill."

There it was...it was her! Once she said her name, I knew exactly who she was. I immediately remembered her from a film I had seen. She was one of the spiritual experts featured in the movie. I had watched that movie a million times. I remembered her especially because she had been the only black woman in the film, and I was excited she had been showcased in it. Now, however, I was floored! I was stuck in a state of disbelief. I was having a difficult time connecting such a positive, life-changing film to this audacious, tactless woman who seemed to have absolutely no principles at all. Without yet having ordered anything to eat or drink, she had already blown into the restaurant like a hurricane, ripping up and tearing apart everything in her path. Surely, this was not the same woman from the film. How could this be?

Mr. Capable Assistant made it clear that Blazing Orange would not be paying Mr. Showtime's bill. Now that the debate was over, I suggested a couple of hand-crafted cocktails for the ladies, and they ordered drinks. When I returned with the cocktails, one of the little ducklings did not like her beverage. I offered her several other cocktails, having to explain in detail the ingredients in each one. She finally decided on another drink, so I took the first drink back to the bar and brought her a new, different drink. She didn't like the new drink either...but she decided to keep it anyway.

I was now ready to take their food orders. But before I could do that, Blazing Orange explained to me that they were in a hurry. The three of them had to be at the airport in a short while, and they wanted me to assure them that I would be able to serve them in time. I assured the ladies that I would take excellent care of them, that I would make sure they made it out in time to make their flights. Even though the restaurant had just been swamped by the outlet of Mr. ShowTime's event that day, I still had no doubt that I could make this happen for the ladies. Instead of focusing on what to order, they reiterated how they could not miss their planes and made a huge deal about how important it was that they get service immediately. However, when I finally began to take their entrée orders, to my surprise, they first wanted another round of cocktails *and* appetizers. Sensitive to the timeline, I suggested that I should just ring in all the food at once—second round of drinks, appetizers and entrées. This way, everything they ordered would be prepared right away. Blazing Orange told me no. It was totally fine to bring out the appetizers first.

I was confused. They had just demanded I expedite everything and made all this fuss about being in a hurry, yet they had time for another round of drinks and coursed out appetizers. Some hurry... I rang in the second round of drinks and the appetizers in the computer system. Then, I made some moves around the restaurant to check on my other tables—and, of course, to check on Mr. Showtime. While checking up on the other tables, at least three different servers approached me and said, "Hey, the lady in the VIP is looking for you." I was thinking to myself, "Wow...I just left out of there like three minutes ago, how could she ask for me through three different people that damn fast?" It was difficult to imagine one of the ladies getting up out of her seat, opening the closed door to the VIP room and flagging down servers who were passing by, but this is exactly what happened. I hurried back to the VIP room to conquer the matter. They wanted to know why their food was taking so long.

What?

I rushed into the kitchen to check on the apps. I used my charm with the cooks to expedite the salad and the crab dip they ordered. When I dropped off the appetizers a couple of minutes later, they were then complaining about the entrées. Apparently, the service was too slow for them. They felt they should have had the entrées by now. Remember, I offered to ring in all the food at the same time, but Blazing Orange refused. She wanted the appetizers to come out first. Now she wanted the entrées, just when the appetizers had come out. Meanwhile, the same duckling that didn't like her cocktail but wanted to keep it, didn't like the crab dip either, but rather than send it back, she wanted to keep it too. Impatient and agitated, they asked me to just have the entrées boxed up to-go. However, because I had placed a "rush" request in the computer on all the food they ordered, by the time I got to the kitchen, their entrées were already plated and ready to be picked up and delivered to them. But now, they wanted it all boxed up to-go. I did not want to be responsible for them missing their flights. At this point, however, Blazing Orange and her special crew were so completely full of themselves that their actions threatened to destroy the entire afternoon and make a mockery of my excellent service standard.

Like a Jedi, I rapidly retrieved all necessary to-go-ware for the ladies—to-go boxes, napkins, plasticware and plastic bags. I quickly de-plated the food and transferred it into to-go boxes. I placed all the neatly packed food in the plastic bags with the napkins and plasticware—separate bags for each separate order. Because she had complained about them, I had little duckling's unsatisfactory cocktail and disliked crab dip removed from the ticket. I printed out the check and dropped off the to-go entrées with the bill. Together, the three of them only spent about $85. All they had to do was pay and jet. I was excited to be done with them.

I left the ladies and headed straight back to Mr. ShowTime to check on his party. They were finished eating, and it was just about time to drop the bill on them too. When I pulled out the check presenter with the bill inside, Mr. Capable Assistant asked me to also give him the bill for Blazing Orange and her party of three. I hurried to the computer, reprinted her check and took it back to him. Naturally, I headed back to the VIP room to tell the ladies the news. When I opened the door to the VIP room—lo and behold—the three ladies were sitting there at the big conference table, eating the entrées right out of the to-go boxes!

As if they had all the time in the world, no one was worried about a single flight leaving the city. They took their time eating, then demanded more sauce, more ketchup, more this, more that. Another drink, another refill. More water. After eating half the meal out of her to-go box, the same duckling who had earlier sent her drink back, sent her food back too. And they were obnoxiously loud. In the comfort of the VIP room behind a closed door, separated from the rest of the restaurant, they ate without regard for etiquette or manners, like they were at home on the floor watching television. They were exhibiting behavior that would have been completely unacceptable in front of others, yet they had no problem doing it all in front of me. It was as if my lowly disposition as server made me invisible to them, and it did not matter that I witnessed them being so inappropriate. Undoubtedly, Mr. Showtime had no clue these ladies were there, instigating such confusion in so close proximity to him, attempting to attach themselves to his celebrity. Would they have behaved this way had they been added to his party? Probably not, but I was glad I had made no attempt to include them.

I had already totaled their bill and handed it off to Mr. Capable Assistant. As soon as I'd informed them that someone else was paying their bill, they wanted to order more shit. Who does that? And what the hell happened to the big hurry everybody was in? At this point, I felt used, abused and disgusted.

The ladies took their sweet time finishing up their food. When they were finally preparing to leave, I mentioned to Blazing Orange that I had seen her in the famous inspirational film. She, in turn, tried to sell me a 12-Step program. Despite the awful hurry she was in during the entire lunch visit, she spent the next several minutes telling me about her 12-Step Program and how I could get it at a special price if I hurried and signed up for her online seminar. Blazing Orange reached into her bag...instead of giving me money for a tip, she gave me her business card and insisted I go to her website to sign up. My disdain level grew from disgusted to flabbergasted. Although she told me my service was great, I felt insulted by the fact that, after acknowledging her as a reputable spiritual leader, she attempted to *sell* me something. She was supposed to be paying me money for my services, not the other way around. I could not help but feel her representation as a spiritual person was fraudulent.

At this point, the rapid pace at the restaurant had slowed down a bit. I made my rounds to secure my other tables. After offering a very gracious thank you to Mr. ShowTime and his party, I returned to the VIP room to an unbelievable scene. Blazing Orange and her posse had left the previously exquisite room in absolute disarray. They had moved and rearranged all the table settings. The table was a two-dimensional dumpster, toppled with nasty used to-go boxes, silverware, plasticware, cloth napkins, paper napkins, left-over food, plastic bags and disorganized fancy place settings.

Despite there having been only three of them, six or seven chairs were completely out of place. Food was all over the floor! It looked like the room had been ransacked by a small mob of toddlers. And to my dismay, Blazing Orange and her crew, after demanding to sit with Mr. Showtime uninvited, after lying about being in a rush, after running me all over the restaurant, after having had items removed from their bill and the rest of the bill paid by Mr. Capable Assistant, after leaving the room in chaos, left me not one red cent to tip me for my supposed "great service." Not a dime.

This story is the perfect example of how self-important some black people believe they are and how their dismissive mentality is pervasive across educational, economic, and apparently, even spiritual lines. Promoting oneself as an expert in spiritual guidance would suggest that one would know how to behave in a restaurant. In some psychologically dysfunctional way, for black folks, the values of respect and dignity become warped in this arena. Those plagued with self-importance seem to lose all sight of everything except themselves.

Manipulation

It's like...black people want all of their reparations back, right there at the dining table. They want everything America owes their ancestors, and they want the restaurant to give it to them. Always...without fail, they want something for free. The consistency with which this happens is truly amazing.

For any and every possibly slightest inconsistency they can find, they want a discount. They complain that the meal was not hot enough, so they want a discount. They complain that the meal "tasted different last time," and they want a discount for that. If it took too long to be seated, they request a discount for that. Each of these issues is possibly worthy of a discount, but black folks lie about these things to get what they want. When the bill arrives, with a straight face, they will swear a certain item never made it to the table, so as to avoid paying for at least one thing.

The restaurant sells lemonade. It's printed on the menu. Sometimes, black folks want lemonade but simply refuse to pay for it. They already have water and sugar on the table. Instead of paying for lemonade, they ask for extra lemons and then proceed to make their own lemonade right there at the table.

Oftentimes, black folks show up to the restaurant with a gift certificate or some other promotional discount. Problem is, they never read the information on the certificate, or they misunderstood the promotion. So, they show up to get something for free, but they show up at the wrong time or on the wrong day. Or, they show up and find the promotion has expired. Many black folks become upset with the server or angry with the restaurant when they refuse to honor the expired certificate or when they cannot make an exception for the misunderstood promotion. If they had simply read the fine print, they could have spared themselves the time and everyone else the trouble. Black folks become so obsessed with getting something for free that sometimes they completely overlook the pertinent details.

Once during a shift, a party of five sat down for lunch. One person in the party had downloaded an app on her cell phone which would give her a discount on the lunch meal. At some point during the lunch, she showed the other four in the party how to download the same app to receive the same discount on each of their meals too. Everybody was so busy trying to get the discount that no one had actually read the promotion, which indicated *only one discount per table*. Had they shared one check, they could have simply used the discount for the entire bill. That way, everyone would benefit from the deal. However, because they had requested five separate checks, only one of them could use the discount. Rather than accept the fact that they could not use the discount as expected, they began to fuss among themselves over who should use the discount. Then they became upset when the restaurant would not make an exception for them. Again, had they read the details of the promotion, they could have avoided ruining their nice lunch with an unnecessary argument.

Sometimes black people make costly requests, then they don't want to pay for the things they asked for. For instance, a guest will order a cocktail and say, "Hey, make that a double." At that time, they are not considering they will be charged double the price for the double drink. Or, the guest will request a side of shrimp or a lobster tail to accompany an entrée, then later argue with the server about the amount of the bill. A double cocktail, a side of shrimp or a lobster tail can add $10 to $20 each to an already hefty tab. Many times, black people do not think about this when they order, and the prices smack them in the face when they get the bill. Rather than accepting the fact that they must pay, they fight for a way out of the situation—through manipulation, dishonesty, deception.

There are even times when black folks will call the restaurant long after they have left and complain about a meal that was perfectly enjoyable, in order to get the money for the bill credited back to their debit card. It is almost as if, after having thoroughly enjoyed such a wonderful meal, they get home and fret over how much money they spent on the bill. So, they call the restaurant seeking a way out of the payment.

Most trifling of all is when black folks eat more than half of the meal they ordered, then send it back. They will make up ridiculous charges about the food to have it removed from the bill. Too cold, too hot, too salty, too spicy, too bland, too sweet, undercooked, overcooked, too big, too little, sudden imaginary food allergy, sudden mysterious illness. They find clever ways to avoid paying the bill. Black folks will even take a strand of hair from someone's head sitting at the table and put it on the plate, and subsequently complain there was hair in the food. This happens all the time.

Servers have seen it all before. Servers have heard every line and seen the game spun from every angle. Somehow, shiesty diners seem to think that when servers are extremely busy, they will not remember what is happening at each of their tables. On the contrary, it is during the busiest times that servers are most on top of their game. They remember dropping off the red potatoes to the lady in the blue dress. They also remember watching her eat them while they were refilling her water. So, they smile and nod when the lady in the blue dress insists she won't pay for the red potatoes because she never received them. Lying about the red potatoes may be a small deal to the lady in the blue dress. However, *The Case of the Missing Red Potatoes* will create extenuating circumstances and unnecessary confusion between the server and the management and could take hours to resolve.

Servers know when guests are being dishonest. They know all the tricks. The hair-in-my-food trick. The black-pepper-in-my-drink trick. The dish-never-made-it-to-my-table trick. Servers know the difference between a guest who is genuinely dissatisfied with something they ordered and a guest who is lying to have the bill reduced. They do this all day, and the games are nothing new to them. They have seen such scandalous situations so many times that the lies become pathetic and predictable.

This massive insistence on getting something for free stems from an inherent fear among black people regarding money. Shameless acts like those mentioned above highlight the fact that many black folks are preoccupied with money, or the lack thereof. The choices they make at the restaurant are economic, financially-founded, fear-based decisions. After generations and generations of stretching a dollar to survive, black folks wage war on simple things like lemonade, even when they can actually afford it.

The making of one's own lemonade at the table is a psychologically-twisted survival tactic. The bitterness of black life has given black folks plenty of *lemons*. They are mentally programmed to make lemonade—to take something sour and make it sweet. At the restaurant, this metaphorical anecdote for survival plays itself out in reality, in the actual physical world. Ironically, someone brought them real lemons, so they made real lemonade.

Why pay for lemonade when it can be enjoyed for free? This concept only makes sense to a person encompassed by fear—trying to save a dollar, trying to have a good time while trying to survive. Many black people exist and breathe only in survival mode. Survival mode is not a switch that can be casually flicked off and on. Because black people use survival strategies so constantly in everyday life, it is difficult to turn off the survival mechanism and overcome the fear of spending money. And spending money on something unnecessary like a fancy dinner merely makes the difficulty worse. The fear becomes more pronounced, more exaggerated in the overpriced restaurant environment, whereby everything the guest orders has to be carefully considered by its price-point from a survival perspective. If black folks would only take an honest inventory of their restaurant behavior, it would be apparent that survival mode is not serving them well. It is causing more harm than good—not just in the restaurant but in life in general as well.

KASSONDRA ROCKSWELL

THE SIX THOUSAND DOLLAR BILL

It was a Saturday night in Atlanta, and I was working at a restaurant downtown. I was informed there was a reservation for a party of 60, and I was asked to lead the team of servers that would take care of them. I immediately shied away from the opportunity. I thought to myself, *who makes a reservation for 60...who does that?* Normally, the appropriate way to have a gathering for a party this size is to reserve a banquet space large enough to accommodate everyone in the party. Then the group could enjoy catered food or a special menu and dedicated service from a small group of capable servers. Someone had made a reservation for a party of 60 as if it were simply a reservation for a party of six. Even worse, I was working at a restaurant which allowed such foolishness. No respectable joint would allow a reservation for 60 people without requiring them to book a special section for themselves.

The small restaurant was open for business as usual that evening. It was already packed with other patrons. There was nowhere for one group of 60 people to go. How was this supposed to happen exactly? Sixty new people are about to bum-rush the restaurant...and then go where? Then, there was the important matter of payment. I was in no way interested in splitting a bill 59 ways for the 60 ladies in this party. The restaurant was already incredibly disorganized and horribly managed. Serving 60 black women there, at one time? No way.

Just as I was building my resolve to stay out of this potential mess, I was then informed that the party would only last from 7 p.m. to 9 p.m. and that there would be only one check for the entire group. Okay...two hours? One bill? Plus, there would be an automatic 20 percent gratuity added to the bill. We would make enough money on that one party to enable us all to go home afterwards without taking more tables. It was guaranteed money *and* a chance to go home early. I decided to go ahead and lead the party.

More news staggered in—new developments regarding the party of 60. As it turned out, one of Atlanta's popular reality TV stars was coming into the restaurant to join them. She was hosting a weekend celebration for women, and these ladies had flown into the city from all over the country to participate in her event. Some had driven to Atlanta from as far as North Carolina to take part in what was a full weekend of female festivities. My restaurant just so happened to be a Saturday night dinner stop on the agenda for these ladies.

Just like the incident with Mr. Showtime, restaurant staff was always happy to see a celebrity up close and in person. So, of course the restaurant became filled with excitement at the news that she was coming through. She was, after all, an R&B icon. Besides, everyone was wondering if she might bring her husband, so they could see him too. So yes, everyone was looking forward to her arrival.

To my surprise, the 60 ladies all showed up around the same time. Now it was time to deal with the immediate problem. There was nowhere for them to sit, remember? Well, they ended up scattered across the entire restaurant—six here, eight there, twenty in the VIP room, another fifteen over there, seven more somewhere and four squeezed over yonder. I divided the crew into sections based on the weird seating configuration, and we all split up to cater to the scattered party.

Everything was complimentary for the 60 guests. They ordered from a special prix fixe menu—all included with their trip to the restaurant. Ms. R&B-TV was featuring her very own new brand of alcohol, complete with eight original cocktail recipes. Meaning, our bartenders had to create eight different specialty cocktails for her 60 guests, using Ms. R&B-TV's new alcohol. The problem was, the managers were clueless about what was going on. Apparently, they didn't expect the alcohol and were not prepared to serve it. And no one had discussed these surprise drinks with the bartending staff. Ms. R&B-TV's people just showed up with the liquor and the recipes. And literally, that's all—liquor and recipes. They did not supply anything else. They brought no ice, no juice, no mixers and no fruit to help make the cocktails. This meant that all the ice, juice, mixers and fruit was supplied by the restaurant, at the restaurant's expense. On top of all that, the cocktail recipes were complex—requiring muddling of fruit, mixing of juices and shaking of contents. Our bar staff was hard-inclined and ill-prepared to create these unknown cocktails with no warning, no heads up. They were great bartenders, so they adjusted. They muddled, they mixed, and they shook the drinks into quasi-premium cocktails. The ladies were able to keep ordering cocktails until the last bottle of the featured alcohol was gone. And they did. They tried every cocktail recipe until the bar eventually ran out of ice, juice and fruit to serve its other customers.

The ladies ate, drank, and became merry. They were extremely pleasant and gracious to the staff. When she showed up, Ms. R&B-TV was just as delightful as the guests had been. She took pictures with everyone, with anyone who asked. The chef sent her what she ordered, then in addition, sent her a huge complimentary platter of the same thing. She ordered more food and several drinks for her private entourage—the three ladies who had walked in with her. They ate good and enjoyed everything.

As the evening settled, the large group trickled out of the restaurant full and tipsy, having had a wonderful time with good food and great service. I packed up the remainder of her platter in a to-go box for Ms. R&B-TV, and she and her personal crew left as well. For such a large group, the encounter had run incredibly smoothly. There was nothing left to do except run a financial report for the event and finalize the transaction. After doing exactly that, I went to look for Ms. R&B-TV's People. Ms. R&B-TV's People was really only one person, a black woman who appeared to be a possible assistant to Ms. R&B-TV. She was the same one who dropped off the liquor and the recipes earlier and insisted the bartenders make their cocktails. She was also the one who made the reservation for the party of 60. And she was the one who was supposed to pay the bill. However, the lady was becoming somewhat elusive.

Each of the servers from the crew, including me, kept walking around the restaurant in circles looking for her, doing the Chi-Lites dance.

Have you seen her? Tell me, have you seen her?

She was taking her time, enjoying the live music, chatting with other guests, sipping her cocktail. She would leave the restaurant and go outside to chat for a spell, then come back in and walk right past one of us. Although it was tempting to just snatch her up by her weave, we had to remain professional. We were trying to get a credit card from her, the same one that she was supposed to whip out to pay the entire bill. However, she was in no hurry to finalize this transaction. The situation started to feel more and more weird. She was obviously evading us intentionally. Why hasn't she paid yet? Why won't she just pay?

Another hour or so passed. Each time one of us approached her, Chi-Lite would continue her conversation with someone else without any acknowledgement whatsoever. And when I walked up to her and said, "Excuse me," so we could address the matter, she told me she would be with me in a moment. She was being very passive-aggressive, nice-nasty. We tried to get the management involved, but they were moving at the same turtle-like pace as Chi-Lite. The server crew for the event was way past frustrated. We had cleaned and reset the entire VIP room, as well as the other areas the ladies had occupied. Because we had committed to the large party of 60, we had been assigned no other tables, no other guests to serve. There was nothing left to do, so we were all pacing around, ready to go home, waiting for her to settle the bill.

The restaurant was filled with beautiful people and lively music, however, the music and the people were so loud that it felt more like a nightclub than a fine restaurant. Perhaps she was lost in the club-like ambiance. Surely, she wasn't just avoiding us, avoiding payment. We were in denial. At this point, we had simply dismissed her as possibly too inebriated to think straight. We had split up like a SWAT team, scouring the entire joint to triangulate her location. Finally, one of the servers from the crew came back to me and informed me that Chi-Lite said there was stuff on the bill that she did not order. "Bullshit," was my reply. I took the receipt over to Chi-Lite and meticulously explained each item in question one by one, as professionally as I could, as aggravated as I was.

> *Ma'am. The crab legs and all these entrees right here, plus these drinks here were all ordered by Ms. R&B-TV. The four Vodka and pineapples, you ordered personally, remember? You had one, you requested one for Ms. Snobby Mobwife Reality Show Lady who was sitting next to you, then she asked for another remember? So yes, you had one, she had two. Okay, the*

> *fourth one you ordered was for the white gentlemen who showed up after everyone left. You know, the white guy who had on the baseball cap? Also, these two desserts, you asked me to bring those out to the security guard...remember, I packed the desserts in to-go boxes for you, just like you asked me to do. Is there anything else I can help clarify for you?*

Without hesitation, she began a game of make-believe. Her version of the facts obviously happened in a parallel universe. First off, she was still in complete denial about how many cocktails she had ordered. Or, she was just too drunk to remember. Then, she insisted that everything Ms. R&B-TV had ordered was supposed to have been complimentary. She argued that the desserts she had personally ordered for the security guard, he was supposed to pay for those himself. But of course, Mr. Security had already left the building—gone. Then she began to ramble on about how the bill was much more than what she had agreed to with the restaurant. Once they realized how serious the issue was, management finally became officially involved.

Bringing management into the situation was not just to expedite a resolution to the problem. Involving management was important to the staff for other reasons. At a well-structured, organized restaurant, the management knows what dishes left the kitchen and which drinks left the bar. They know which server picked up what, and they know where it was delivered in the restaurant. They have systems in place to ensure this. In a dysfunctional, disorganized restaurant like this one, however, no one in management is certain about anything. If the lady swears she didn't order something, the restaurant will not likely have protocols in place to ascertain the truth. As a result, places like this often hold the server responsible for the item(s) in question. As far as management is concerned, the server could have deceptively rung up items on the customer's bill for their own personal consumption. Restaurants which operate like this one don't really care what happened to the item, as long as the money for it does not come from the restaurant's pockets. So, they will make the server pay for the items and take the money for the items out of the server's pay. There was no way in hell me and my crew were footing any portion of Chi-Lite's bill. We weren't having that.

Here was the deal. The prix fixe menu from which the ladies ordered was $69 per person. Multiplied by 60 women, plus the additional non-prix fixe items, including entrees and non-complimentary cocktails, plus desserts, plus tax and automatic 20 percent gratuity, the bill totaled somewhere around six stacks. The first gesture by management to help resolve the matter was to remove several items from the bill. They removed about $400 worth of food and beverages from the bill. This brought the bill down to somewhere around $5,600.

During the interim of waiting on management to handle the situation, I walked around the restaurant a few times to check on the progress of the transaction. The first time I walked through the venue, I noticed a couple of managers talking to Chi-Lite at a cocktail table near the front entrance. They were attempting to be patient with her and maintain their professionalism. I waited about 10 or 15 minutes, praying they'd all be done soon. During the second walk-through, I noticed that Chi-Lite and the management had moved from the front of the restaurant to the VIP room in the back. Every single member of the management staff on shift that night was in there. The general manager, two assistant managers, the chef, the owner, and the owner's two adult sons all had Chi-Lite surrounded at a table. It looked like a restaurant scene from a mafia movie.

Management had quickly lost patience. They were obviously arguing over the bill, and they were drawing attention from the entire staff, as well as the many patrons still enjoying the food and music. The hot-head owner lost his cool. The ordeal became so heated in that VIP room that the owner of the establishment actually drew his fists at the woman! Had his two sons not held him back, he might have struck Chi-Lite in the face. Again, I waited, just hoping this whole shit would come to an end so that I could get my money and go home. However, the third time I checked for a status report, I found the VIP room completely empty. When I went looking for them, they were all standing *outside* the front of the restaurant, arguing with Chi-Lite on the street. All of them were out there—all the managers, the chef, the owner, his sons and Chi-Lite—and a police officer had pulled up to the scene...blue lights flashing and all.

I stood there, paralyzed by the display of ugliness. A black-owned restaurant had called the police on a black woman, and they were outside quarrelling on the street in a historically celebrated black neighborhood. I was awestruck. By this time, it was after midnight. My team and I were pissed. We had no tables and nothing at all to do. We had been waiting to settle the bill with Chi-Lite for almost three hours, and we still had not been paid. Despite the contract she had signed and the agreement that was made, she refused to pay what she rightfully owed. This was totally unbelievable.

Once I had seen the police there, I was done. I had no more patience to wait and see whether or not Chi-Lite would be going to jail that evening. I had to be back at the same restaurant in less than 9 hours to open up for brunch. I decided to leave and just get paid the next day. I was ready to go home. And, so I did. When I left around one o'clock in the morning, they were still arguing with the police out front.

The restaurant grapevine is very small. Word spreads very quickly. When I arrived to work the following morning, Chi-Lite was front page restaurant news. The entire brunch staff was aware of what had happened with Chi-Lite, even those who were not there the night before. Everyone was in disbelief that the police had to be called on a patron because she refused to pay her extravagant bill. Even though it was clear that Chi-Lite was the one who had caused all the commotion, the final story floating around was that Ms. R&B-TV had brought 60 guests to the restaurant and left without paying the bill. After all, it was *her* event. It was her name and her pictures plastered on everything. In Ms. R&B-TV's defense, however, she may not have been aware of the stunt Chi-Lite pulled at the restaurant. She had already left hours before, and everyone from that event was long gone, except Chi-Lite. No one was certain if Ms. R&B-TV was aware of the tomfoolery taking place in her name. Whether this was a one-woman show or one with a supportive cast, it remains a mystery.

What we do know is this. Chi-Lite was only willing to pay $4,000 of the $5,600 total bill. It was around 2:00am when the restaurant management acquiesced to the $4,000 settlement, but they demanded the payment be in cash. Chi-Lite agreed to pay the $4,000 cash but then, however, pulled out four separate credit cards and told management to swipe each one for $1,000.

Later that week when I returned to work, management asked me if I still had all the receipts from Ms. R&B-TV's event because they needed to make copies of them. Naturally, I asked them why. Management needed to fax the original receipts to the credit card companies. As it turned out, Chi-Lite, after settling with management upon $4,000 for the total bill, then paying with four separate cards at $1,000 each, had called her credit card companies and disputed all four charges to the cards.

3

BLACK FOLKS DON'T CARE

Exploring Apathy

Not Giving a Damn

It's not what you look at that matters, it's what you see.
—Henry David Thoreau

The ambiguous behavior of black folks in the restaurant environment makes them appear completely indifferent about the experience. Amidst the attitude, indecision, distrust and all the other factors explained in Chapter 2, the consensus regarding black folks on the matter is that they simply don't care—about anything. They don't seem to care about the restaurant, the food, and certainly not the server.

Disdain

Cleaning up behind others has never been deemed respectable work in American society. Those who must perform the tasks of cleaning up after others have historically been looked upon with the collective contempt of society's negative judgement. Americans hold with esteem those jobs which can be rightfully deemed careers, and successful careers are those that start with a college education and end with high-paying salaries. It takes no advanced degree to learn how to deliver an entrée or clean a table. Out of all the choices of what one would like to be when he or she grows up, no American child ever stood with pride and exclaimed, "I want to be a servant!" Forbes confirms in online data from 2015 that children dream to become doctors, astronauts, teachers and firefighters (Adams, 2015). No American child wishes to grow up and be a butler, a maid or a server in a restaurant.

For black people in particular, the feeling towards servant work is distinctively contemptuous. The American slave narrative, still so fresh in the collective memory of the people, has played a crucial role in the way black people feel about servants and all servant-related work. Having been *forced* to cook and clean and step and fetch for others as slaves sheds a dark light on any job reminiscent of these duties, as well as the people assigned to them. Public opinion declares that folks with better options for employment would choose more "respectable" work. Hence, the consensus regarding being a restaurant server is that one would only be a servant because life had *forced* him to be, because he could not aspire to be anything greater.

Once slavery was over, and black folks were no longer limited to slave work, they aspired to achievements in education, science, law, religion and medicine. Once black people began to re-master these other disciplines, they kept moving forward and never looked back. Servant work has been openly regarded with absolute disdain ever since.

As much as things seem to have changed, they have remained the same. Service jobs are still considered jobs that no one wants to do. In the eye of the general public, service jobs are undesired, bottom-barrel work, reserved for the poor, uneducated and unintelligent. The disdain for the individual is directly connected to the job. Although the service industry is full of intelligent, highly educated people from a variety of cultural and economic backgrounds, those people are judged by the duties they perform. By mental transference, service is not only an inferior job, but the servant, as well, is an inferior person. Peculiarly, the same person who is worthy of respect while sitting on an airplane or shopping at a grocery store becomes invisible when they are working at a restaurant—disrespected and dismissed just because of a change in setting.

Disregard has abusive tendencies. It is selfish and inconsiderate. It ignores the server. It forgets the server is a human being. It runs the server all over the restaurant like a robot. Disregard is the absence of caring. Although the server provides the caring that makes the great time great, that care is often unappreciated and unreciprocated. It discourages valued employees from doing a fantastic job with every table, every time.

As black folks have advanced American culture and thereby assimilated into it, the historical notions regarding class and servitude have been deeply embedded into the psyche of the people along the way. One would think that, because black folks have endured such horrific discriminations, they would be more empathetic to the plight of the service worker. However, the evidence proves just the opposite to be true. For those black people who are disconnected from power in most aspects of their lives, the dining experience offers them the opportunity to finally sit in a position of power and demand things from another person. In doing so, they exhibit the same oppressive behavior of those their ancestors once served. They are automatically disrespectful to the service worker. Then, there are those black people who cling dearly to their advanced degrees, their social status and their income levels. In doing so, they uphold and perpetuate the social constructs of status and class. Within this elitist frame of thinking, it is easy for them, even if subconsciously, to look down on the service worker, just as those their ancestors once served looked down on them.

Human respect should be automatic. Just as skin color should not disqualify a person of the right to dignity, neither should a person's occupation. It does not matter what a person's job is or how one earns his pay. Being human is about respecting other human beings, as individuals, each with his own story, each with a unique, beautiful path in life. Despite the never-ending American quest for financial success, making more money never makes one man greater than another. All work is respectable and has significance, regardless of the wage value our society has placed on the job. As well, all people are worthy of respect, regardless of their job titles.

Disconnection

Think about it. What is the purpose of going out to eat at a nice restaurant? Is it merely...to eat? Why do people dine out anyway? Why doesn't everybody just cook at home and eat at home? Why the need to actually go out somewhere and risk having a terrible meal and horrible service in a room with complete strangers? Of course, there are some folks who eat out because they can't or don't want to cook at home. For the most part, however, people go out to eat for ultimately one reason—to have a nice experience.

Just as people choose to visit the movie theater rather than stay at home to watch the movie on the sofa, people choose to visit restaurants for the same reason. Whether people acknowledge it or not, when they choose to go out, they are choosing to venture into the world and interact with others, to engage and to be engaged by others who share the planet. In doing so, they interject themselves into the currency of life. Dining out gives people the excuse to get all dazzled up and wear their best clothes. They go out of their way to look their best because they know they will be interacting with the world. Although they may not be talking to every patron in the restaurant, they want the pleasure of the company of strangers. They want to be surrounded by conversation and laughter and the meetings and conventions of others. If they do go out somewhere, and hardly anyone else is there, they feel a sense of loneliness. They would rather other people be there too, so they can share the vibrant energy of a room full of people, even though they may not speak to them at all. Dining out at a restaurant is one of the most popular ways people gather to share this wonderful human experience.

Black folks are an enigma in this regard. Many dine out to share this experience with the world, but then go very far out of their way to create disconnection. It is natural to want to be connected to others, however, black diners often struggle with this concept in the restaurant arena. They express this desire in contradictory ways.

Just like disvalue, disconnection can be abusive as well. Through disvalue and disconnection, people can simply become invisible. They are there, but no one values them enough to truly see them. As a result, it becomes easy to condescend them, ignore them and dismiss them. Here's an example. A server is walking past a table with her hands completely full. She has no room to carry anything else. However, a guest stops her, trying to hand her a few more dirty plates. The guest does not see her. Not really. It is utter disconnection. Or, when a guest yells out for more ketchup to a server who has his back turned, rather than waiting to talk face-to-face, the guest does not see him. Or, a server approaches the table to deliver the food, but before she can put any food down on the table, the guest is demanding extra condiments and refills. The guest does not see her. Not really. The guest recognizes a servant figure, that is all. The guest does not truly see a person. They don't see a human being, worthy of one's best behavior. This type of shameless disregard is a result of disconnection from the experience.

Black folks go through the process of getting dressed up to dine out, consciously knowing they are going out into the world to have a great time. They look so impressive when they show up—stunning, actually—yet they are often detached from everything but themselves. They are truly apathetic about the entire dining experience, but they look fantastic. Although the way they look on the outside appears to exude confidence, the way they behave shows a complete lack of such. They look so rich, yet they behave so poorly. It appears the only thing they gave significant thought to, was the outfit they chose to wear. They do not at all consider the many other important variables of the evening which deserve a little thought and attention.

Figuring the Rest Out Later

It's like going out to purchase a nice car while only focused on the car note itself—thinking that, if one could afford the car note, one could afford the car. There are other important factors to consider like car insurance, gas costs, automobile maintenance and the possibility of parking/traffic violations. Yet, to a person clueless about buying a car, not one of these issues may have crossed his mind at all. As long as the car note gets paid, the rest must be figured out later.

Some black folks apply this same methodology to many things, and there is no exception when it comes to dining out. Just like with the car note analogy, they choose a nice restaurant. As long as they can afford the meal, everything is all good. They do not consider the possibility of appetizers, dessert, tax, gratuity, parking or possible valet. The meal *may* get paid, but they must figure out the rest.

This means that many black people go to the restaurant prepared to only pay for the food—the basic meal. Without considering tax and tip, this almost always results in a money shortage when it is time to pay the bill. It is reminiscent of the age before debit cards and split checks, when everybody shared one bill and paid for their food with cash. Black folks would dine in a group, and the cash would always be several dollars short when it was time to pay the bill. In obvious confusion, each person at the table would look to somebody else as the short-changed culprit, when in reality, it was everyone. This was because each person at the table only calculated the price of the meal. No one dared to include tax and tip, so the money was always short.

Only thinking about the basic meal makes the dining experience unnecessarily awkward and complicated. What about the appetizers, the dessert, the tax, the tip, the parking, the valet? What happens when a diner is not prepared to pay for these things? Well, under these conditions is when appetizers and desserts become mysteriously dissatisfying so they can be removed from the bill. Since the tax must be paid, the tip may be significantly shorted. Or worse, the person may not leave enough cash to cover the entire bill, much less a tip. And parking? Without preparing for parking, patrons might spend an extra 45 minutes searching for a free place to park before they even make it to the restaurant. And in the case of parking service, black folks never seem to be prepared to pay the poor valet. Often times they will actually ask a server to give them some cash, so they can have money to pay the valet when they leave. The inquiry sounds a little something like this,

> *Hey, do you have any cash on you? Can I add, like, an extra three dollars to your tip on my debit card...and you give me three dollars cash so I can pay the valet?*

For the record, the practice of asking a server for cash is discouraged by most management at fine dining restaurants and may be subject to disciplinary action. Additionally, a cash tip does not equate a debit card tip, as debit card tips are subject to additional fees, taxes and tipouts. A server can be shorted through such an exchange. And, even more still, asking a server for cash is just tacky.

The fact is, there is too much afterthought and scuffling to figure things out. When black folks are in the mode of figuring out the rest later, they are constantly hustling. They are scrambling to make things happen at the last minute, often at the expense of everyone else. It is inconsiderate of those who serve, and it sabotages the experience. It is foolish to expect great service and a great experience without any contribution to one's own wonderful time. A little more thought and preparation can create a better connection to the entire experience and be completely wholesome for everyone—on all sides.

FUNNYMAN'S UNFUNNY FAM

I had already served Funnyman and his girlfriend twice at the restaurant. He was famous, and the manager wanted to impress him, so I was asked to take care of him personally. I was a fan of his comedy and was accustomed to watching his standup work on television, so I was happy to serve him. Now I had the honor of serving him a third time. This particular visit was for a party of about 20 guests, reserved in the VIP room for Funnyman's birthday.

The party was comprised of Funnyman and his family. Everyone was well-dressed, but there was something strange about the group. They all trickled into the VIP room and sat in complete silence. Nary a peep from anyone...which was weird because they were all family. I offered them drinks. No one wanted a cocktail. I explained the specials the restaurant was offering that night. No one had any questions. Complete silence. Everyone just sat there, sipping water. It was so awkward. In fact, no one said much of anything at all, until one lady asked me if I could turn on the television in the VIP room so that they could watch the television show, *Empire*. Suddenly, the entire room slowly rose from the dead in agreement with this request.

Excuse me, what?

Here it was, Funnyman's birthday...but there was no funny. There was no positive energy, no kindness in the room, no joy, no laughter. No one had even taken a photo to commemorate Funnyman's birthday. They had met for dinner with a reservation for a special, private room in one of Atlanta's most popular dining spots, yet they wanted to watch a new late night drama on primetime TV. For a moment, I wondered if Funnyman was playing some type of prank on me. Afterall, he was a comedian. I looked around for hidden cameras. No such luck. They were serious as hell.

They wanted to watch TV. It seemed as if they were of some religion that didn't allow alcohol, conversation or photos—just television.

For some reason, the managers could not get the television in the VIP room to work that night. Funnyman's family could not watch *Empire*, and they were highly disappointed. The dinner arrived and everyone ate in silence. It was really strange. The possibility of watching *Empire* had brought hope to the room. There seemed to be some real connection among them through the television show. Perhaps the show could have broken the ice in the room and sparked spirited conversation and laughter. Now that *Empire* was not an option, the room had returned to its cheerless, dismal state. It was a bit odd to be serving a famous comedian and his family on his birthday in a room with absolutely no laughter.

Later, when it was time to pass out the checks to the party—split checks, of course—Funnyman pointed out to me about five or six folks who would be included on his bill. He confirmed that the rest would pay for themselves. I split the checks accordingly. When I returned to the VIP room to pass out the checks, the guests who had been seating in seats one, two and three were gone. All three...gone. No joke. Could all three of them have gone to the restroom at once? This was not funny.

I turned to the lady in seat four and asked if she knew what happened to the three ghosts. She then called out to someone way over in seat 16. After an entire evening of silence, I was surprised she could speak so loudly. She initiated an inquiry something like this, which echoed through the room four or five times through four or five people,

> *Hey, where JoJo Nem at?*
> *Did they leave?*

I don't know.
They left?
Umph.
Is they comin' back?
Hey yall, where JoJo Nem go?
No tellin' where they went.

The focus of the family dialogue was based upon where JoJo Nem *had gone*. No one was concerned about JoJo Nem's *return* except me. I was working at a restaurant with management that would try to force servers to pay for guests' unpaid meals out of the server's own hard-earned money. I needed to know where the hell JoJo Nem was so that they could pay their bill. And if JoJo Nem weren't coming back, then I needed to know which one of them was taking care of JoJo Nem's bill. There was no way in hell JoJo Nem's food was coming out of my tips. Where were these people?

At this point, everybody was good and full and ready to go. Funnyman was now ready to leave, so he asked me to settle his bill. I ran the split payments of all the family members in the party. I ran Funnyman's credit card—the total bill of all those in the party for which he chose to pay. When I returned to drop off the payment receipts, the family was still having the discussion about JoJo Nem. This time, the echoes which rang throughout the VIP room sounded like this,

Was you supposed to pay for them?
Naw...I thought they was gone pay for theyself.
Did they just leave and not pay nothing?
Maybe they thought Funnyman was gone pay.
Umph.

Apparently, the echo of JoJo Nem's whereabouts had not yet made it back to Funnyman. He was signing his payment receipts and still had no idea what was going on.

I re-approached Funnyman and inquired about the disappearing act of his three ghostly family members. Funnyman was confused. "What?" he exclaimed in disbelief. To smooth over the awkward moment, I apologized for the confusion—as if it was somehow possibly my fault that his peeps pulled an eat-and-run. The entire family chimed in at Funnyman all at once, reiterating the same echoes from the previous few moments. As if watching an active tennis match, I stood in the middle of the room amongst Funnyman's family. With my head jerking from person to person, I followed the ranting of each family member like a tennis ball flying back and forth across the room.

They must've slipped outta here fast.
Umph.
We don't know where they went, Funnyman.
Was you supposed to pay for them?
I didn't even see 'em leave.

Funnyman, obviously embarrassed and shaking his head, pulled out the same credit card—*again*—and asked me to swipe his card a second time for JoJo Nem's food. As the family filed out of the room to leave, their focus was only on JoJo Nem. Everyone was so preoccupied with their disappearance that, out of a group of 20-something folks, no one dared bother to say thank you...except Funnyman. I wondered if he might use this evening in a future standup routine...*I Can't Take My Family No Damn Where*. It was perfect comedic writing material.

Disvalue and disconnection can make an evening horrible for everyone involved. It is impossible for people to be connected to the dining experience when they would rather be watching television or on their cell phones. As with Funnyman's family, they were physically present, but mentally somewhere else. They preferred watching people on screen to engaging with real people sitting next to them. It's as if they were intentionally looking for something to help them zone out and disengage from the situation. This is baffling in a public place, even if in a private room. They were supposed to be celebrating, however, they were completely disconnected from the notion of celebration. Not only were they disconnected from the restaurant experience, they were disconnected from each other as well. To be fully present in the moment means focusing on the current real time experience. It means enjoying what is right in front of you, not missing out on the beautiful moments. It is remembering that life is always happening in the now.

Breaking the Rules

Black folks are exceptional. The rules do not seem to apply to them—ever. Understandably, many bend the rules simply out of habit. Within the black culture, people are so accustomed to working things out, so used to making a way out of no way that this methodology seeps into areas where it is completely unnecessary. An example from a different realm of service may offer better insight into this issue. Take black folks out of the restaurant arena and put them in a rideshare environment. Even here, it is almost always black folks who ignore the regulations and cheat the system.

The rideshare game is very simple. A person needs a ride to go somewhere. Through his mobile application, he can choose a fare to ride all by himself. Riding by himself, he can also choose to add a stop along the way. Or, for a cheaper fare, he can choose a shared ride in which other riders may join his trip along the way. A shared ride has limitations. A rider cannot add a personal stop along a shared route because other riders may join. With a shared ride, the rider must indicate how many people will be getting in the car. This is important. First of all, it allows the app to charge slightly more for multiple people. Secondly, it lets the app know how many more people it can possibly pick up along the way. No matter which type of ride is chosen, the rider has only a couple minutes or so before the driver is prompted to cancel the ride and move along.

Black people do not care what the app says nor how the app works. This creates inevitable problems and unnecessary conflict. It is usually black folks who are often not ready when the driver arrives, and they expect the driver to wait past the allotted wait time. It is most often black folks who choose the shared ride for the cheaper price and then lie about how many are riding. When the driver shows up to pick up one person, instead there are two or three people. The driver who has driven all the way for the pickup will be forced to:

> a) accept the ride, break the rules and screw up his route and his money, or
> b) cancel the ride.

It is a total waste of time for everybody involved, including the other passengers who may have already been in the car on the way. It is a waste of time and gas for the driver. And on top of everything else, whoever called for the now-cancelled ride and must now call and wait for another driver. It's a total loss. Other times, black folks will choose the shared ride for the cheaper price, and *still* ask the driver to make multiple stops along the way. Time is money. Gas costs money. The driver does not get compensated for all these extra requests, and almost certainly won't be tipped by the person asking. Even worse, the rider may actually have the nerve to become irate with the driver if the driver does not comply.

This tenacity for rule-breaking applies to many aspects of black folks' existence—the restaurant is certainly no exception. Just like with the rideshare experience, many black folks are wired to identify each and every loophole/scapegoat/hookup in a restaurant situation and use it to their advantage. Why must the rules be broken? From whence does such madness come?

It's the American way.

The American nation was built on disobedience and rule-breaking ideology. Many of its early settlers were criminals and prisoners, ejected from Europe during a time before prison buildings existed, when exile was a legitimate form of penal punishment (TheHowardLeague.org, 2016). When the United Kingdom found itself overwhelmed with criminals, the government just shipped them off to their colonies to get rid of them.

Somewhere around 50,000 criminals were transported from Great Britain to America during the mid-18th century before the Revolutionary War (BBCNews, 2006). Yet even before then, criminals had already penetrated American soil. History teaches that some of the first English settlers sailed to America, fleeing from their homeland in fear of being persecuted and executed for their religious beliefs. However, many who were shipped away were murderers and thieves, guilty of crimes unrelated to their religious faith (Barnes, 1921). Some of these same settlers battled and murdered the very natives who taught them how to survive in the new land. Our country was birthed at the expense of the entire Native American population from whom its vast territories were taken (Biography.com, 2016).

These criminal settlers would become the forefathers and leaders of the American nation. The American ways of life—its ideals, customs, institutions, religious beliefs, structures of government—all originate from people the English thought best to expel from their general population. So, America has existed as a rule-breaking nation since its very inception. Its creation story is one of crime, exile, trespass, theft, war—and deceit, as it re-writes history to cover up the misdeeds of its forefathers. To this day, America is an unapologetically gangster country—breaking the rules without penalty or repercussion. This is the legacy America has left for its future generations to overcome.

From American culture, black folks have adopted the attitude of breaking the rules. And just the same, they expect to break the rules without retribution or consequence. It is learned behavior, justified by trying to survive in America. The restaurant world just so happens to be the perfect arena for black folks to practice the

American art of rule-breaking, without certain penalty. Hence, the rules in that arena are bent until they are broken.

When dining, it is the norm for black folks to lie, cheat and steal—all under the guise of survival. There are instances whereby black folks shamelessly take things from the restaurant that should remain on the table. It is commonplace for items to come up missing. They take the cute little stuff off the tables, and they take them home. Silverware, salt and pepper shakers, sugar caddies, ramekins, tea kettles—these things disappear without a trace. Although it may be improper to say anything about it to the guest, well-trained servers are very aware of everything going on in their sections, and they know when things have been taken from their tables. And they know who took them.

There is an unwritten consensus among black people, a collective responsibility to *stick it to the man,* and it is warranted by the historical slave narrative. Capitalism has disparaged folks for so long that many black people truly feel unsympathetic towards cheating capitalistic entities. For black people, this is a matter of subconsciously-enforced reparations and karmic serendipity. However, as black folks believe they are only taking advantage of the establishment, this is untrue. While they are stickin'-it-to-the-man and shitting on Big Brother, real hard-working people are getting hurt. Breaking the rules, and then doing so with absolute disregard for others, can result in catastrophe.

HOLIDAY HELL – FROM RESTAURANT TO JAIL

A group of black folks in Coral Springs, Florida, went out to dine at Big Bear Brewing Company in the middle of December 2014. It was Christmas season and, like most restaurants, Big Bear's interior was decorated for the festive holiday. The party of 13 ate up good food and drank up good drinks. During the course of the evening, the party repeatedly sent food back to the kitchen, complaining it was not cooked properly—all the while still ordering more food. They did the same with the drinks as well, complaining they didn't taste good.

However, when the bill arrived, several members of the party had issues with the amount on the receipt. They complained about the bill. They had racked up over $350 worth of food and drinks. Uncertain as to which specific excuses they provided to management, the management proceeded to discount the bill to appease the group. The resulting bill was nearly half the amount of the previous bill, now approximately $180.

According to Lieutenant Joe McUgh, one of the Coral Springs officers on the scene, things went haywire when it was time to pay. Instead of tipping the server appropriately, the group left her some coin change (NBC6.com, 2014). Insulted by the disrespectful gesture, the female server refused to accept the tip and walked away. Apparently, when the waitress refused the insulting tip, it pissed off the group of black folks in the party and they threw about 15 cents worth of coin change at the waitress (NBC6.com, 2014). As she walked away, a few of the members of the party followed the server into the kitchen. Another server who was in the kitchen tried to intervene, at which point two black men from the group attacked the employee, striking him repeatedly until he fell to the ground, after which they struck him in the head with a glass beer mug.

The group then proceeded to destroy the restaurant. According to the police report, one of the black female ringleaders picked up a glass, then went into the kitchen and threw it at an employee (Akbari, 2014). Glass mugs were not the only thing they used as weapons. They threw Christmas ornaments around as well. (Seiden, 2014). Lieutenant McUgh added, "Then they began to throw things around the restaurant. They were throwing chairs at glass partitions. They were throwing salt shakers at other waiters and waitresses. It was complete mayhem in that restaurant..." (NBC6.com, 2014). Someone from the group noticed a waitress hiding behind the bar, attempting to call 911, and proceeded to throw a salt shaker at her, (Seiden, 2014). The local police had received multiple 911 calls from restaurant employees who were so scared, they feared for their lives. NBC6 News Anchor Keith Jones reports that police arrived on the scene to find patrons running from the restaurant as if the place was actually on fire, (NBC6.com, 2014).

The co-worker who tried to come to the server's aid in the kitchen, ended up at the Coral Springs Medical Center with serious injuries for which he suffered 13 staples in his head. Management from Big Bear Brewing Company estimated the restaurant damages caused by the riot to be about $2,000 (Akbari, 2014). Most interestingly, when the authorities arrived on the scene, the suspects were still hanging out in the parking lot. They did not feel the need to run from the scene or immediately leave the premises after causing so much destruction inside the restaurant. It is almost as if they thought they had done nothing wrong or felt justified in their behavior—breaking the rules with no expectation of retribution or consequence. Because they were still there when the police arrived, they were pointed out by the restaurant staff and arrested on site, right where they stood, still in the parking lot. Police escorted the four ringleaders, two black men and two black women, off the premises and hauled them off to jail for various charges of assault, battery and disorderly conduct (Seiden, 2014).

During an entirely separate incident in May 2016, four other people were cited in a different restaurant catastrophe in the Atlanta area, during the celebration of another highly-observed holiday. At Kiku, a Japanese steakhouse in the city of East Point, Georgia, a black woman beratingly asked a busboy what he was smiling about. He replied that it was his job to smile. The woman's brother then got up out of his seat and punched the busboy in the face (Habersham, 2016). The chaos that ensued as a result has become one of the most shameful dining incidents in black history.

In an online video that went viral after its posting by others in the restaurant at the time, a war can be witnessed taking place between plain-clothed guests and uniformed restaurant staff. They are all in a state of disconnected rage, throwing plates, boxes, carts and punches at each other, hurling large trays across the room like medieval weapons—all while supposedly celebrating Mother's Day. The entire ordeal was completely insane. First of all, a patron struck an employee in the face with his fist. Secondly, the employee struck back. Then, more employees—both male and female—joined the fight and exacerbated the battle. Meanwhile, the other black patrons in the restaurant, completely disconnected from the fight, took the opportunity to walk out of the restaurant without paying their bills—using the fight as the perfect excuse to not pay for food, nor tip the staff. And to make the matter even more pathetic, the host of one of the captured videos, commentated the scene with laughter, hysterics and buffoonery. All of these people were black folks.

As a result from the chaos, restaurant owner Charlie Son suffered approximately $5,000 in damages between physical injuries and unpaid bills (Jensen, 2016). All this violence, ensuing from a black woman asking a young black man what he was smiling about. What kind of smile could it have been? Was it a killer smile? A mischievous smile? Sly, sneaky? Lustful? A crooked one? What type of smile warrants a punch in the face?

Interestingly, Mother's Day is the busiest and craziest day of the year for any restaurant. Despite the entire country's choosing to do so, it is not the ideal day to dine out. It is so extremely busy, so frantically hectic on Mother's Day that restaurants take huge shortcuts to make it through the ordeal. The quality of the food is compromised. The service is rushed. The staff is stressed out. The menu prices are escalated. And everybody at every table wants extra special Mother's Day spa treatment. Any restaurant open for business on Mother's Day will have its rooms filled with tension, anxiety and impatience, coming from all angles. This is no excuse, however, for punching a worker in the face.

Black folks have been struggling for hundreds of years to achieve a true sense of respectable dignity. Yet, every day in restaurants across America, there are black folks who do things to deny other black folks this lasting impression. In this particular case, it is four black men and one black woman—all captured on tape in what appears to be their church clothes—wanted by the police for "battery, theft of services and inciting," (Artz, 2016).

During the two most respected holidays where folks should be celebrating the spirit of love—Christmas and Mother's Day—instead there ensued hate in the form of material destruction and physical violence.

4

BLACK FOLKS DON'T EVOLVE

Exploring Stereotypes

Pigeon-holes of the Patron

Those who do not move, do not notice their chains.
—Rosa Luxemburg

No one likes to be stereotyped. People believe they are exclusive as individuals, that no one looks or acts exactly the way they do. People like to be noted for their uniqueness as individual beings. This is why, historically, the American people have fought the notion of stereotyping, or classifying any particular segment of society into one group. It has always been important for humans to recognize each person as a unique individual. However, when one group behaves so badly, so consistently, so collectively, in the same environment, it makes it difficult to dismiss notions of stereotyping.

Black folks have been behaving the same way for so long when they dine out, that they have ultimately created stereotypes for themselves. As much as they may not like to admit these truths about themselves, the behavioral characteristics they exhibit as a group of people are very real. Most of the generalizations made about them are based on hard evidence and absolute undeniable fact. The people who observe them see the same behavior continuously repeated, over and over again, and can't help but feel the same way. After only serving for a short time, any server can easily notice a trend and a pattern developing among certain groups of people. As much as one would like not to profile or stereotype individuals, it becomes obviously apparent that many of the profiles and stereotypes are absolutely true.

In *Waiter Rant*, Steve Dublanica also takes note of how, over time, dining behavior can become quite predictable among patrons. "Since tipping is a social behavior, it should come as no surprise that patterns emerge regarding how people tip," (Dublanica, 2008). Like it or not, black people have been distinctly categorized based on certain characteristics like age, gender and status, as well as sexuality, and yes, race. It has reached the point in the restaurant industry where black folks' exceptional dining behavior is easily foreseeable and grossly unoriginal to waitstaff. Restaurant staff can pretty much make correct assumptions about how black people will handle their dining experience before they even sit down at the table. It is a sad reality.

Of course, within each stereotype, there are exceptions. There are some who do not fit any of these stereotypes at all. There are black folks who defy all stereotypes and dine with excellence. They don't want trouble. They are focused on a great time. They smile, they dine, they tip, they leave. The issue is, however, that cases like these are exceptional and happen only rarely.

There are others who want so badly to avoid these stereotypes, that they go far out of the way just to prove they represent something else. They order food that really *should* be sent back to the kitchen, but they never send it back because they know black folks endlessly send food back to the kitchen. They do not want to be categorized into the group who does this. These are the black people who tip well, despite the bad service they receive, because they want to represent themselves appropriately, as something non-stereotypical. Again, this scenario is seldom seen. This is how the stereotypes manifest, and this is why the stereotypes exist. Most black people act the exact same way under the exact same circumstances.

Grouping black folks all into one big box is an easy automatic default. If these notions of stereotyping are to be dismissed, then the stereotypes must be proven untrue. If black people want not to be subject to the existence of the stereotype, then they must have the propensity to be something greater than the stereotype itself. The behavior must change to represent what is true. This way, the stereotypes are diminished and the truth is exalted.

As it stands right now, there is much work to do.

The Black Male
Stereotype: impatient, needy, flirty, passive-aggressive, callous, cheap

Black men are interesting characters to serve. Black men are ever-mindful that they are black men, and many of them wear their struggles on their sleeves. They begin the table interaction with their fists up, ready for war. Refusing to smile, the black male is tough and often abrasive in the way he asks questions about the menu and orders his meal. He is attempting to set the tone of the dining experience by displaying an attitude of strength. Rather than simply requesting a refill on his beverage, he may make a sarcastic remark about the bar, "Yall run outta dranks back there?" He wants to appear to be in control, but he comes off as impolite and arrogant.

To female servers, black men can especially aggravating. Rather than simply enjoy a female server's great service, many black men consistently approach the dining situation as a mating ritual. His constant flirtations make the server uncomfortable. In this regard, he has desires and expectations from her service that have little to do with the restaurant. He becomes oblivious to the fact that she is at work, that she has other tables to serve. The other tables she is serving are just like a phone call she put him on hold for, until she returns to the primarily more important conversation with him. Every time she walks by his table, he needs something else or has more questions to ask and more conversation to offer. He becomes possessive, needy and impatient—like a lover instead of a diner.

The Black Female
Stereotype: abusive, dismissive, pretentious, tactless, disrespectful, incessant, demanding

Ask any server, and most will agree that black women are the worst diners to serve. Most black women are simply too high-maintenance in the restaurant to be enjoyable. Many black women carry a bad attitude like an expensive handbag—something worthy to be shown off. They act as if it is en vogue to be inconsiderate of other people. The constant demands, the shameless attitude and the iffy tip help secure black women a spot on the top of the list of *Worst Customers to Serve*, while simultaneously winning the award for *Most Likely to Ruin a Server's Day*. Of course, this stereotype does not apply to all black women. But again, so many behave so badly that the behavior ultimately represents the entire group.

Whether it be cutting the server off before he can finish a question or spending her entire time at the restaurant on her phone, black women seem to be completely comfortable with rudeness and disrespect. It does not matter whether she is visiting from corporate America or from the neighborhood, her behavior is the same, regardless of income or socio-economic status.

On far too many occasions, black female servers have run back into the kitchen, screaming mad, pissed off at what some black woman did or said at the table, demanding an answer of other black women in the kitchen,

> *What the hell is wrong with us?!?*
> *Why it's always gotta be us, clowning like this?*
> *Black women are fuckin' crazy as hell.*
> *What happened? I bet she was black, wasn't she?*
> *This bitch at Table 12 got me fucked up.*
> *I can't fuckin' stand black women.*
> *If I go back over there, I'm gonna get fired today.*

All these rantings come from the frustrated minds and cursing mouths of other black women. Black female servers have refused to go back to a table of black women to finish serving them. Black servers have even chased them down after they've left the restaurant to ask them about a lousy tip. It is so difficult not to call them bitches when they leave.

Despite the collective struggles of black women, despite the history that binds black women together, sadly there is no automatic camaraderie between them at the dining table. The natural connection they normally share in other environments is completely lost here. It is because the black female diner looks upon the black female server with disdain rather than with respect. In this regard, the black female server is no longer an ally and cannot be embraced as a sister or a friend. All the diner sees in the server is someone who is beneath her.

Blacks in Numbers

After considering the individual stereotypes of the black male and black female, imagine the inevitable situations that occur when these two are together, or when they multiply in number to form a group. All the character traits of the stereotypes can be swirling together at once. This can be overwhelming to someone providing service.

Occasionally, a server will encounter a happy black couple or respectful group. They sit down and have a great time. They smile and share laughter. They share food and wine and enjoy themselves. Then, they tip great and leave. Most often though, a server will encounter a simultaneous variety of negative stereotypical behaviors from black couples and black groups.

For instance, whether it be a bunch of church folk, a book club or a family, a group of older black women can often require the highest level of maintenance. When they dine, they are simply more polished models of the younger black women whom servers despise. Instead of being loud and rude, they offer a more reserved version of wrecking one's nerves. They act entitled to whatever they want because of their age, and they do not care how anybody feels about it.

With their quiet sense of authority, they can be even more unreasonable, more worrisome than their younger counterparts. They need so much attention. They complain about absolutely everything while they are satisfied with absolutely nothing. They criticize the menu. The criticize the food. They criticize the restaurant. They take their sweet time. They overstay their welcome. They study the bill like it's a trigonometry exam. They complain about the size of the print. They question the charges. Some tip. Some don't.

The collegiates, however, are a little different. Remember, college students live on a very small budget. They are accustomed to surviving off tacos and burgers from paper wrappers and plastic bags. Hardly ever do they get to eat real food served on a real plate. When they choose to have a fine dining experience, they know they really can't afford to be there.

For most of them, they are living away from home for the very first time, and they are spending from their very first real-life budget. In college, money is funny. It does not stretch like the plastic bag that carries a student's fast food meal. So, when the collegiates so happen to splurge on a nice dinner, there is hardly any splurging at all. They may not have enough loot to cover the tip. Or, they may simply be afraid to spend next week's budget in one hour on one meal. Or, they may just be brand new to the restaurant game and clueless about what is expected. Regardless of the reason, for the bulk of them, the tip is usually short—way short.

Nevertheless, the collegiates do not ask for much. They tend to be reserved and quiet. They stay low key and try to have a nice time. They never overstay their welcome. They eat and run. Perhaps they have too much studying to do, too much life to live to stay in one place too long.

Couples can be often peculiar. Couples don't realize how certain interactions over dinner, or the lack thereof, reveal so much about their relationship to a stranger. Some couples may be new to each other—feeling weird and being awkward. Other couples have been together so long, they have nothing to say. They sit through the entire dinner without saying a word. Others may be somewhere in the middle of an argument. She orders. He orders. Somebody makes a telephone call. The other fumbles through screenshots. No sweet conversation. No lively debate, just awkwardness and discontent.

Sometimes, couples are simply unhappy together...period, and they bring all their issues with them to dinner. The unsuspecting server gets swept right in, having to maneuver around the madness, trying to delight people who were already unhappy when they sat down. How can they enjoy the meal if they can't enjoy each other's company? It's an impossible task.

Elderly couples can be weird and awkward as well. Black folks from older generations have a unique disposition at the dinner table. They vividly remember the Civil Rights Movement of the 1960s. They were there. They lived the cruelties that are difficult for most to watch on television. They know firsthand what it is like to be unwelcomed in restaurants.

Interestingly, even though 50 years have passed since the height of the Civil Rights Movement, at dinner they still sit in silence, seemingly apprehensive about their existence there. It is almost as if they expect the restaurant management to march over and tell them they don't serve black people. They remain quiet and reserved, intimidated by the ambiance and overwhelmed by all the fuss.

For many of them, the fancy restaurant is foreign territory where everything is so unrecognizable it may as well be written in Mandarin. This makes it difficult for them to interpret the menu. They do not always understand the descriptions of the food because they are unfamiliar with the language of the cuisine. Additionally, they are often confused by the pricing and the unique way it may be presented on the menu. They get thrown off by the fancy lingo, the technical menu design and the swirly script or font selection dancing across the page. Many times they need visual help just *seeing* the menu.

Most black elderly couples just want a simple meal in a nice place. They care very little about all the luxurious ambiance and the complicated cuisine. They want easily recognizable food like steak or chicken at an affordable price. An expensive bill can take them by surprise, rendering a tip out of the question.

Gay and lesbian couples bring a unique dynamic to the dinner table. Generally speaking, gay men—no matter what color their skin—are treasured guests at the restaurant. They are welcomed for their understanding and appreciation of great service. They are typically happy, bubbly and festive, and they tip well. When they show up as a pair, they usually have a terrific time. Two gay men dining together at a restaurant—lovers or not—usually exemplify the epitome of dignity and respect. However, when gay black men, in particular, arrive as a large group, they show up and show out. Serving them evolves into something altogether different. In a group scenario, they become very difficult to serve. When gay black men gather in large numbers, they somehow lose their morals and manners and operate as a gang. The same lovely gentlemen dining as a party of two can turn into high maintenance divas when dining amidst a large group of gay black men. The dinner situation can swiftly transition into a fiasco of dissatisfaction, a step-and-fetch-it soiree.

The black lesbian couple is a unique exception to the basic negative stereotypes of the black female. The couple tends to be quiet, reserved, introspective—never abrasive or loud. However, the reserved demeanor seems to be attributed to or connected to social insecurities connected to their sexuality. They appear to be looking for discrimination, waiting to be slighted. They are preoccupied with their sexuality and they think everyone else is too.

In an article written for the Anxiety and Depression Association of America, Dr. Brad Brenner explains that members of the LGBTQ community suffer from anxiety and depression at a rate up to 2.5 times higher than their heterosexual counterparts (ADAA.org, 2019). Dr. Kevin O'Grady of the LGBT Center Orange County agrees, exploring the reasons behind the higher-than-average anxiety rates. He identifies high levels of daily discrimination and persistent prejudice as the culprits.

> *Twenty-nine states still offer no protection against workplace discrimination based on sexual identity, and 32 states offer no protection against discrimination based on gender identity...As a result, 52% of the LGBT population live in states that offer*

> *them no protection against workplace discrimination. Imagine the anxiety created by knowing that if your boss found out about your sexual orientation, you could lose your job. Unfortunately, this kind of anxiety is reality for the majority of our country's LGBT population* (Anxiety.org, 2015).

Much like racial discrimination, discrimination based on sexuality and gender identity forces the population to walk around shielded—on constant guard—so accustomed to discrimination that they stand armed for war, ready for battle. Though reserved in demeanor at the table, many lesbian couples are watchful for any signs or possibilities of sexual discrimination. It is completely understandable why they may be uncomfortable in environments where they believe their sexuality or gender identity might be an issue. The fine dining restaurant environment, with all its hoopla regarding traditional service and conventional principles, is certainly a place of potential discomfort.

MR. MA'AM

One night, while working at a Buckhead restaurant near Lenox Mall, two black women sat down for dinner at one of my tables. One of the ladies was extremely feminine—soft and curvaceous. She had a long weave down her back, and she was wearing a pretty pink dress which matched her long nails and fully made-up face. The other lady, the taller of the two, was obviously a woman but carried the full appearance and disposition of a man. She wore slacks and a plaid button down, and she sported a low-cut fade. By the way they interacted, it was obvious they were a lesbian couple. I greeted them and introduced the restaurant in the same usual way—with a happy smile and a genuine, warm welcome.

I walked up to the table and said something like, "Good evening ladies. How are you two doing tonight?" When I said the word *ladies*, the masculine woman jerked her head up from the menu and gawked at me like she wanted to punch me in the throat. I quickly realized that I had offended her, but I was confused as to why. I stood there and maintained my composure. After introducing the restaurant's featured entrée to the two of them, I walked off in a complete state of frustration. Something inside of me knew with certainty that she had been offended by the word *ladies*, yet I had no clue whatsoever what word I was supposed to use otherwise. The big plaid long sleeved hunter's shirt the lady was wearing did not hide the supersized triple X bosom she had nestling underneath. I felt, just because she was dressed like a man did not her a man make. To me, she was clearly a woman. What the hell was I supposed to call her...*Mister*? Address her as *Sir*?

In no way did I want to offend this woman, yet I was somewhat confused by the fact that she seemed to be insulted by my best intentions, and I was frustrated at the disconnection that stood between us. My eyes registered two women, regardless of their apparel. To assume the woman considered herself a man, just because of her choice of dress, to me, in my mind, *that* was disrespectful. How could I assume anything otherwise? Why would I? How would a server know when a guest affiliates with an identity outside of the societal norm?

Most fine dining restaurants put their servers through an extensive, rigorous training process. An important part of this training is learning how to greet guests according to the restaurant's standards. There is a specific focus on addressing each guest by using the "proper" prefixes: Mister, Miss, Missus, Sir, Ma'am, Lady, Gentleman. These references are so important within the restaurant culture that one can be reprimanded or terminated for not using them. Servers are taught to use these labels religiously. Although there should be, there is no training at all that focuses on sexual identity and gender fluidity. No lessons are taught on how to respectfully serve members of the LGBTQ community. Whatever was happening in the LGBTQ community, I clearly was not getting the memos. I wanted desperately to rectify the situation as best I could.

I spent the remainder of my time serving those two ladies, trying my best not to use the word *ladies*. I danced around pronouns, replacing any feminine references with *you*, or *you all*. It was awkward and obvious, having to think of different words to use or omit in order to accommodate them. I had not been prepared for such a reality check that evening.

Because of the misnomer mishap, I went above and beyond the call of duty for the two of them. The food arrived on time and perfectly plated. I made sure every drink was filled and refilled. I carefully wiped down their table between each course, making sure to not leave a single crumb in sight. As the evening progressed, the ladies smiled and laughed, seemingly enjoying the meals they ordered. When I discovered that it was Lady-in-Pink's birthday, I brought complimentary dessert for both of them to enjoy. I even had the manager stop by their table to offer birthday salutations. When they were finished with their meals, I graciously packed up their leftover food to-go for them.

I had hoped maybe, just maybe, we had recovered a connection, and all was forgiven. However, when they left, they left me nothing. Lady-in-Plaid had paid the bill by debit card, and when she signed for the bill, she left the tip area completely blank. She made sure to fill in the total at the bottom, which was only for the exact amount of the bill—no tip included. Woe was me...I was in denial. I figured she must have left me the tip in cash.

I searched all over the table, looking for money. I looked up under the plates and dinner napkins. Nothing there. I looked under the table to see if perhaps they left cash that had fallen on the floor. I even asked the managers if they had picked up the tip from the table on my behalf. All this unnecessary investigation was to no avail. They had spent over $100 on dinner and left me no tip. Nothing. It was a clear message that they were dissatisfied. I felt horrible.

On a different evening at the same restaurant, I approached one of my tables to greet a young, white guy. He was a slim dude, not quite 6 feet tall with short, dark, spiked hair and several facial piercings. He was casually dressed in a thick, plaid long-sleeved shirt and black jeans. I walked up to the table and happily offered, "Good evening, Sir."

We exchanged salutations and small talk. He was very polite, and he enjoyed his meal. He left a nice tip and skedaddled. However, moments after he left, I was approached by my manager, who was obviously shocked in amazement. She was awestruck and devastated that I called her fiancé a man!

What ever in the world was she talking about? I figured she had me confused with some other server. I was genuinely clueless. Although many servers at the restaurant had met the manager's fiancé, I had yet to meet her, until just now apparently...on this particular evening when she sat alone at a table in my section with her spiked hair. I had no idea. I didn't know she was a woman, much less the manager's fiancé.

There was nothing about this woman that would indicate she was a woman. In fact, it appeared that she had put in a great deal of work to *not* look like a woman. I never questioned once whether or not she was a man. She was dressed like a man. She acted like a man. She looked like a man! There was no trace of womanhood anywhere. She had decidedly wiped away all traces of womanhood to embrace masculinity and manhood. How could she be offended that I called her *Sir* when she had embellished her appearance to look the way Sirs do? She had intentionally chosen an appearance to look like the opposite sex, and she had done a great job at it. Yet she was offended by the fact that I couldn't see through the disguise?

And the party I served with six gay black men and one black woman...where the gay men became offended because I served the lady first? As I dropped the food in front of her, I said in the most delightful tone, "For the lady..." To my surprise, all the men erupted into sudden exclamation:

Uh, she ain't the only lady.
Why we can't be ladies?
Shit, I want my food first too.
We all ladies at this table honey.

At most fine dining restaurants, especially in the South, it is customary that the lady at the table always be served first. What's a server to do? Or say? When a woman who is obviously a woman does not want to be called a lady? When a woman who appears to be a man wants to be referred to as a woman? When a group of gay men insist they are ladies? How do we respect the multi-faceted choices in transgendered identity under the current restraints of a two-sided gender world?

In the absence of a surgical procedure to officially define oneself as a different gender, in the absence of a name change to make this transition clear, how does the rest of the world know what to call those who identify with a different gender? Through the clothes they wear? And just because one wears clothes identified with the opposite gender, does it automatically mean he or she is transgendered? No, it does not.

The issue is that we live in a world that expects us all to choose, explains Kate Bornstein in her book *Gender Outlaw* (1995), "a world that insists we be one or the other." The world is still so black and white—boy or girl, man or woman, Sir or Madam. New vocabulary must be created to accommodate these evolving ideas, and more dialogue is necessary in order to nurture and respect all alternative lifestyles. Meanwhile, as society makes its way through the conversation and discovers the definitions, mistakes will be made along the way. Hopefully, the misunderstandings will lead to greater understanding, which will progress to tolerance, appreciation and love. People want the right to choose—not to be forced to choose. American culture must allow itself to redefine itself for these changes to take place.

5

BLACK FOLKS DON'T TIP

Exploring Service

Planet Hospitality – The Bizarre and Peculiar World of Food and Beverage
About Servers – Fallacy vs. Fact
The Tao of Tipping

Service to others is the rent you pay for your room here on earth.
—Muhammad Ali

PLANET HOSPITALITY

THE BIZARRE AND PECULIAR WORLD OF FOOD AND BEVERAGE

The restaurant is like a small, independent country. It has its own language, its own social culture. It has its own belief system, political system and its own government. And just like a small country, it exports goods and services at the highest cost for maximum profit. Money is its religion. Because of their oligarchical, totalitarian-type methods, restaurants are stressful places to work. They attract certain types of employees because it's a crazy world that requires special types of people to work there.

Amidst this host of characters are those who are stuck in their lives somewhere and others desperately trying to get somewhere. The restaurant industry draws in both the creative spirit and the cubicle-phobic masses—people who desire the freedom to walk around, people who like talking to other people, people who don't want to swivel in an office chair all day. It also attracts people who have schedule limitations and people who prefer to make quick money, legally. This is why the industry is chock full of students, artists and single mothers. In Waiter Rant (2008), Steve Dublanica sums up this same point, offering, "...the restaurant business is a haven for people who don't fit in anywhere else." Regardless the point of attraction to such a workplace, it takes a unique mental ability to endure the high-paced, random craziness and the never-ending delirium that takes place in a typical restaurant day.

The entire industry is a vulgar, profane environment of the most extraordinary magnitude. Many of the realities inside the restaurant world would leave most Americans spellbound. Compared to the sneaky, backhanded practices often witnessed in the corporate arena, the no-holds-barred, in-your-face disrespect of the restaurant industry can be extremely more brutal on the human psyche.

Underneath all the pomp and circumstance, the elegant appeal and the luxurious atmosphere of a really nice restaurant lies another layer—an awfully ugly one. It is a parallel world full of muck, debris and disgusting filth...as poorly managed and as drug-infested as a dilapidated apartment building in the worst ghetto. It is the dark side of the industry unknown to patrons, which outsiders never see.

Mysteries of Mismanagement

Because everything begins at the beginning, it is important to start at the top. All restaurant problems start from the top, then move their way down. If the management is shitty, so shall be the staff, as well as the service. It is discombobulating and disconcerting that hardly any restaurant can figure this out.

While the staff serves the customers, the management is supposed to serve the staff. However, this is not the active motto of many establishments. The simple truth is, most restaurant managers have no clue what they are doing. And, if they had a clue, they are so overworked and overstressed that they perform miserably. Because of this, restaurant management is almost always inefficient. Almost always. While unknown to the patron, some of the most expensive, highly acclaimed restaurants are riding the fence between minimum efficiency and total disaster.

In all the experience gathered to compose this book, there was one restaurant—only one—where management was always at work, always on time, always on the floor...actually working. Because of this, the restaurant was quite efficient in its operations, and the service from the staff was extraordinary. However, in order to create such impeccable structure, the management ran the restaurant like a boot camp. There was so much verbal abuse and so many military-type politics. Management would scream at and curse out the staff—oftentimes in front of the customers.

Disrespect and mistreatment were simply the daily norm there. The stress level there was unbearable. Sometimes two or three servers would sneak into the food freezer just to have a word of prayer.

If a server was two minutes tardy, she would be sent home—even if that was her first time being late. The staff would be lined up like a squadron for human inspection. Managers checked the creases in their sleeves, the press in their aprons and the shine on their shoes. They were pop-quizzed on everything from the type of light fixtures in the ceiling to the kind of wood on the floors, then promoted or demoted to a better or worse section. They were constantly monitored and under video surveillance—both onsite and remotely.

The staff would work for 14 hours straight, many times without food. Most restaurants offer a "family meal"—free dinner to feed the employees, typically served before or after a shift. It is almost always comprised of leftovers and crumbs, but it is also high appreciated by the staff. For a staff working over 12 hours on a shift, family meal should be customary. At the end of the night, every restaurant is left with enough food to feed an entire neighborhood.

Most times, however, the managers just throw all the food away—intentionally, on purpose, for spite, knowing that the staff is starving. No one cares whether or not the staff ate...or died. They were so brutal that they might watch a server pass out from feeble exhaustion on camera, then complain to her about the next day in the lineup. The servers were like soldiers in some evil, twisted food service regime. At least in the real military, the soldiers get to eat.

The apathetic attitude there towards food was disgusting. So much good food—uneaten, untouched—is thrown in the garbage. The amount of food thrown away daily by the American restaurant industry is surely enough to feed the homeless and put an end to hunger and starvation nationwide. There are no methods in place for recycling food, rather than simply discarding it so irresponsibly. And it's not just the food that should be recycled. There are no standards in place to recycle paper, plastic, glass, aluminum—nothing. Everything, straight to the trash. It's truly disgusting to see this happening on an industry-wide scale. Throwing away all that food and all those products is senseless, irresponsible, unnecessary and ass-backwards. Restaurants should be held accountable for the huge amounts of trash they create and its effect on our environment. They should adopt more eco-conscious disposal policies, and they should be required to recycle everything possible. They should have systems in place to donate unwanted good food to local agencies and homeless shelters to assist those in need. Period.

Because of this *No Meal Military* type methodology, workers were constantly quitting, many without notice. At one point, nearly 30 employees quit within an 8-week period. The result for the restaurant was a super-high employee turnaround. Employees were quitting every day, so that restaurant was hiring—every day. Until they learn how to respect the staff they have, they will always be searching for new people to work there.

The same happened at a Tuscan restaurant in Buckhead. Employees dropped like flies. It was nothing for two or three people to quit the same day. On average, one person quit about every three or four days. New staff had to be hired every single day. By the dozens, new hires would show up, work just *one* day—only to never be seen or heard from again. The owner of the little place was so abusive and disrespectful to the staff, they would curse him out and walk out in the middle of a shift. There is only so much disrespect people will take before they find work elsewhere. Self-respect and dignity are more important to people than reality television would have everyone believe.

The chef, also in a great position of power, can be the most abusive of all. Chefs, in general, are known to be so rude and so profane and so irrational, it makes one wonder if lunacy is a requirement for the job. It is as if culinary school teaches them how to be weird, diabolical, narcissistic psychopaths—sane enough to make fresh pasta from scratch. As crucial as the position is to the success of restaurant, the chef can be the highly detrimental reason for its failure.

A chef will get frustrated at a situation in the kitchen or an issue with the food and just walk out of the restaurant. Some of them get upset and throw plates across the kitchen. Others throw knives. They take their stress out on everybody in their path. It's difficult to distinguish whether or not they are overwhelmed, underslept, crazy, racist, high on drugs—or a combination of all. They belittle the kitchen staff and berate the serving staff, constantly yelling at everyone and cursing out everybody.

In fact, cursing is so commonplace in the kitchen, *Profanity* has become the official language of the restaurant business. The Chef curses out the kitchen staff and servers. The managers curse out the kitchen staff and the servers. The chef and the managers curse out each other. The server staff curses out each other, then they gather together and curse out the managers and the guests. In the kitchen, some of the foulest, most disgusting, most complex curse-word combinations can be discovered. It is automatically accepted as a norm by everyone in the business, nevertheless, it is a culture cultivated by the chef.

The foul environment the chef creates in the kitchen is equally responsible for the lack of loyal employees. Although chefs have been "notorious for boozing, yelling...Your chef is a manager, just like any other restaurant manager. He should conduct himself in the same way you expect every other manager to behave," (Garvey, 2004). Not all chefs are great ones, certainly not in the personality department, and sometimes not in the cooking department either. Despite the brutal reality, the chef is an essential part of the management team and should always represent as a professional with a dedicated crew.

When people are constantly quitting on a daily basis, it fosters anxiety among the remaining staff—even the loyal ones. They lose their job security, fearing each day at work could potentially be the last one. The entire staff starts to look for work elsewhere.

It is impossible to transition from mediocrity to excellence when you have to continuously focus on hiring new employees every single day. The business must spend too much time and money on the continual renewal of human resources. Restaurants end up just trying to stay afloat, scrambling to hold the ship together. There is no room to focus on improvement or innovation. No room to tweak the tiny imperfections or perfect the small details. Hence, the perpetual mediocrity.

Restaurant owners think they get it, but many have no clue what they are doing. Most owners are focused on money—not food, not people. Just like the Buckhead Tuscan joint, they run their businesses on superficial passion and mediocrity. Many owners need bilingual managers to accommodate a mostly Hispanic kitchen staff. Sometimes this requirement outweighs the need for an efficient, well-rounded manager who works well with others. In other cases, owners just want a drill sergeant or an overseer—

someone who enjoys cracking the whip and looming superficial power over others.

There is an array of management personality types, most of whom make the staff miserable. They range from bullies and manipulators to swindlers and thieves. Some are far too emotional, while others try to show no emotion at all. They also can be petty, immature and full of gossip. They often allow favoritism and partiality to get in the way of professionalism, and they have no problem promoting their friends to coveted, key positions at work.

Managers dip in and out—here one week, transferred the next. Managers don't get along. Managers don't support each other's decisions. One manager says *apples*. The other says *pomegranates*. Servers get caught in the crossfire. No consistency. Disorganization and chaos. Improper scheduling. The restaurant's been open for five years, yet the manager is not smart enough to know its customer base or dining patterns well enough to know how many servers to schedule on a Wednesday lunch. Now there are too many servers on the floor. So, some servers get no tables at all. Some come to work and don't make a penny. A couple of weeks of this nonsense, working with staff accustomed to getting paid daily or weekly, and servers will drop that restaurant like a hot potato. Servers will jet and be working for that restaurant's biggest competitor the next week. Fickle.

There are managers who genuinely care but are under too much pressure and work too many hours to manage effectively. Then there are the managers who simply don't give a damn about the job—at all. There are many of them. They show up late all the time. They are always MIA—on smoke break, left out for a couple hours, unavailable, hiding out while eating free manager food, or, just not in today. They do not care about their own jobs, so they certainly don't care about a server's job nor about any of the concerns of the staff. And they couldn't care less about a customer. Ultimately, the customer's needs do not matter to them at all. They are just at work to socialize and/or collect a paycheck and eat the free manager food. They are so heavily despised that servers fight over the chance to work on the days that these managers are off duty.

They do not believe they themselves are the problem. They believe that the problem is the staff—that they hire from a pool of people who bring the problems. And so, they accept the never-ending cycle of hiring as a norm of the business. Owners, and managers alike, refuse to realize the connection between their abuse, their high employee turnover rate and their inability to be more than mediocre.

If customers frequent a restaurant and discover there is completely new staff every time they visit, it is highly probable that the whole place is completely out of whack. The serious employment issues will ultimately work their way into the quality of their experience *and* their food. The fact is, the abuse of staff is merely a reflection of the restaurant's ability to exploit the customer just the same.

Abuse happens to serving staff, not just in restaurants but in all types of environments. Servers work at country clubs, stadiums, arenas, museums, hotels, universities and private companies. One of the ways servers gain access to these various venues is through staffing agencies who misuse the staff in unimaginable ways.

For starters, most stadiums and arenas use staffing companies to hire some of their staff. However, the staffing companies usually do not have enough manpower to handle large stadium-type events. So, Staffing Company #1 will call Staffing Company #2 and contract more staff from them to fill the void. Meaning, within any particular arena event attended by the public is a huge mix of unknowledgeable, unfamiliar, outsourced temporary staff. They wear the same uniforms, so there is no way to make a distinction as to who works for who or who came from where.

Many of these staffing companies hire employees with no relevant skills and no formal training and send them out to various events around town, totally unprepared to complete the job. The employees who do possess the necessary skills and training get sent to assignments where clients have them doing unauthorized tasks not included in their job description. In some cases, servers get sent out on ghost assignments that do not exist. In other cases, they work shifts and do not get paid. The staffing companies maintain impersonal relationships with the staff by communicating mostly through a smartphone app, making it often impossible to reach them and resolve critical issues.

Many agencies take advantage of the service staff they roster. They only care about the money made from the contracts they sign with their clients. The poor staff just falls by the wayside, suffering from many broken policies and broken employee laws. When this happens, employees find it difficult to make demands of temporary agencies. Because they are just "temps," all their legal rights are obscure and inaccessible. There is no one on the management flow chart assigned to advocate for the temporary employees. It seems nobody cares.

All in all, good management should represent a level of professionalism in all situations—from ordering supplies to communicating with staff, from expediting food in the window to handling conflict. Great management would manifest itself as a team of well-rounded, caring individuals—a combination of both male and female—who work well with varied personalities from all walks of life. *Running a Restaurant for Dummies* agrees by offering the following advice to restaurant entrepreneurs, "managers set the tone for the rest of the staff...They affect how smoothly your operation runs, how your staff controls the chaos and treats the customers, and how much money you'll ultimately make," (Garvey et al., 2004). Again, everything starts from the top, down. A horrible manager can ruin an otherwise profitable and healthy business. An excellent manager can make a great restaurant even greater.

Respecting the staff is essential to the success of any restaurant, any business. Understanding the staff, praising the staff, and encouraging camaraderie among them are rules owners and managers should live by (Garvey et al., 2004). Even more importantly, managers lead best by example. Great managers are able to promote cooperation and develop growth among staff members by having a respectful attitude and cheerful disposition themselves. Respect is about more than just talk. Nice words only go so far. They know that respect is the thread that holds any restaurant together.

Mishandling of Money

A restaurant owner who will cheat his staff will cheat his guests just the same. In many restaurants where the staff is being financially shorted by the owner, the guests are being taken advantage of just the same. Independent restaurant owners tend to do whatever they want to do with their businesses. Because of the restaurant industry's disconnection from standard corporate politics, restaurant managers commit crimes against their staff for which corporate managers in other industries would be immediately exposed and terminated. They run their restaurants however they please, with no regard to industry regulations or legal ramifications.

For example, the Tuscan restaurant in Buckhead cheated its staff out of money every week. The owner simply paid each employee what he wanted them to have each week without any financial records or any system of financial accountability. Each week, payday was a disastrous occasion whereby employees would open paper checks to discover ridiculous amounts of nothingness.

Someone would confront the owner, have an argument about the money, then proceed to storm out of the place. This was a weekly occurrence. The owner would never explain the money to the servers. Any questions about it meant having to endure a heated argument with the owner—which would usually result in a walk-out or an on-the-spot termination.

At this same restaurant, the same owner abused his guests in a similar regard. He would overcharge small parties, by up to 400 percent. The same plate of hors d'oeuvres he would sell to the party for $45 was available on the regular dinner menu for 10 bucks. This owner took shortcuts on everything in his restaurant. His posted permits were long expired. His tables were decorated with wilted carnations, and his kitchen plated hardly-ever-fresh fish. He even reheated and recycled bread from used tables to new unsuspecting guests. Even worse, he would systematically add several bottles of wine to the bill of parties that booked reservations there—wine they did not consume—just to fatten up the final bill. When customers would call to question the bill, he would simply lie by trying to convince them that their party did indeed drink the wine. He would even ask the servers to call the customers to help him lie. To add insult to injury, the wine they actually consumed was likely from a cheaper vintage or completely different varietal than the one listed on the menu.

Owners are not alone. The entire industry seems to strive on crookedness and thievery. Managers steal unscrupulously from the restaurant. Managers *and* chefs take food and liquor and all kinds of inventory from these places. Bar managers and chefs trade food for liquor—meaning, they actually negotiate food and liquor trades with food and liquor that belongs to the restaurant. Sometimes, they trade the food and liquor for drugs. Kitchen staff supply their personal parties and birthday celebrations with stolen food, drinks, tools and equipment from the restaurant.

Managers steal from the servers as well. Managers falsify financial reports and adjust tipouts so that servers payout more money than they should. Those managers keep that extra money for themselves. Some managers do this out of resentment simply because they are jealous of the servers they hire. Often having to work 60 or more hours per week, they hate that servers come in and work for a few hours, then get to leave. They hate that servers get praised by the customers while they work hard behind the scenes. And they loathe the fact that many servers make even more money—off tips, for heaven's sake—than they do as salaried superiors.

In retaliation, they create ways to distance servers from the money they can make. This vindication manifests in all sorts of crooked ways. Many managers have an abusive policy in place which forces servers to pay for food and beverages that customers return. A lady orders a lemonade, then decides she doesn't like it, so she sends it back. An evil manager will make a server pay for that lemonade and any other unwanted items returned by his or her tables. Forcing servers to pay for items that customers return makes the sales report higher, which makes the manager look better on paper. Some even force staff to pay for broken dishes by taking the money directly out of their pay, which saves the restaurant money, which makes the manager look better on paper.

Sometimes crooked managers partner with thirsty servers to implement underhanded schemes. There was a manager at a downtown Atlanta restaurant who on busy nights would take money bribes from customers for skipping them up over all the other waiting customers...reservation be damned. The manager would then immediately seat them in the section of her server partner-in-crime. They would then split the bribe between the two of them. Some managers get caught and get fired for scams like these. Others continue in the business for years, destroying efficiency from restaurant to restaurant and wreaking havoc in the lives of all the staff they manage, everywhere.

Staffing companies and catering companies mismanage money too. They take the tips that belong to the staff. Yes. In many cases, they have policies in place that will not allow the workers to even accept tips. Then in many other cases, when clients include tips in their final payment to the company, the staff never sees it. The tips get confiscated by management—stolen by one manager or divided among a group of them, or recycled back into the company. Hundreds of thousands of dollars, that were intended to be distributed among the serving staff, vanish and disappear. Poof.

Sports fanatics and stadium visitors go out to these arenas, have a great time, spend lots of money on food and beverages. They spend lots of money, tipping the workers at the concession stands. Because hardly anyone carries cash to these events, they make purchases by credit card or debit card and tip the workers on the card. At the end of the night, however, these card tips may be likely confiscated by the arena management—never to be seen again. The explanation the company gives to the outsourced staff is:

> *Hey, our computer system is not set up to pay you credit card tips because you don't actually work here.*

Where does that money go? Unsuspecting arena consumers are tipping the concession staff but have no clue that their money never ends up in the hands of the one intended. The staff is forbidden to share this information with customers. Unbeknownst to the public, they are simply tipping the stadium company, after already paying their ridiculously inflated prices for cheap, health-threatening food and beverages. Some of these arena companies are operating business fraudulently. They are taking money from customers knowing full well in advance that the money will never reach its intended destination—stealing it from the staff and using it for some other purpose.

Servers only accept these gigs because of the potential to make tips, only to show up for work and have they monies confiscated for no legitimate reason and without sensible explanation. It's deceptive and dishonest.

Cleanliness, Next to Godliness

Of all the issues that plague the hospitality industry, the matter of cleanliness is one of the most crucial. There is a huge problem when the kitchen is dirtier than the mouths of the staff who work in it. Ironically, the environment where the proper handling of food is of the utmost importance is where there is the most disgusting filth. In fact, filth is the norm in most of these establishments. Many of the most highly-acclaimed and most highly-visited destinations—sports arenas, museums, country clubs and popular tourist attractions—all share these nasty secrets in common. It is with rare exception that places like these are clean in all areas—from front door to back door, including the kitchen, storage, closets and coolers. Hardly any of them pass the test for cleanliness, efficiency and organization. Black folks' concern for cleanliness by way of requesting hot water to soak their silverware, although seemingly inappropriate, becomes highly warranted in this regard.

At very swanky, expensive, award-winning restaurants, dirty silver is simply not tolerated. Soaking silverware is a moot point because everything there is immaculately clean. However, at your average costly fine dining joint, things may be a little different. Silverware may be only half clean before it is rolled into the dinner napkin. More often than not, silverware comes out of the dishwater still viscid with sauces, creams and various partially identifiable food particles too stubborn to surrender to the hot water from the dish machine. To twist the meaning of the age-old adage, *everything does not come out in the wash*.

In essence, the cleanliness of all the dishes is dependent upon how much the low-paid dishwasher person is invested in his job. If he has a poor work ethic or is being treated badly at work—both extremely probable—the cleanliness of the dishes will reflect this. Simply put, if he is underpaid and disrespected, he may not care enough about the dishes to take the extra steps and go the extra mile to ensure they are clean.

Half-washed dishes get mixed in with the clean ones, then placed on the shelf where clean dishes are stored. A server searching for a bread plate may have to go through a stack of dozens before finding a clean one—one without caked-on, sticky spinach dip or chewed up chicken pieces still stuck to it. It is up to the server to take the dishes back to the dishwasher to be rewashed or to notify a manager. Yet again, if the management is abusive or the restaurant environment is toxic, the server may not care, and the communication will be lost. The server could very well choose to use his fingers to flick the food off the cleanest plate he can find and wipe the rest of it with his apron. The cycle of nastiness continues indefinitely. Abuse puts cleanliness at risk.

Another cleanliness issue of crucial importance is running out of inventory during very busy work shifts. When it is extremely busy in a restaurant, it is common for the restaurant to simply run out of stuff. All the water glasses are being used. All the wine glasses are being used. All the steak knives are out on the tables somewhere. Silverware and glassware are always in high demand. The dishwasher can only wash dishes so fast. Of course, one would think there would be enough inventory in supply to serve every customer on a busy night, with a surplus in storage somewhere for backup. But in most cases, restaurants never have enough inventory in supply to serve their customers efficiently.

In order to keep the flow of available glasses going, servers must search around the restaurant and check the tables for unused or empty glasses. While people are still sitting at the tables, enjoying their meals, servers meander through the aisles, confiscating dirty glasses from the tables so that the next drinks can be poured into them. Customers are waiting. Time is money. Customers, clueless as to why they must wait so long on their drink orders, simply assume the poor server or bartender is to blame. In reality, however, there were just no clean glasses.

For example, when a customer orders a mimosa during a super busy Sunday brunch and there are no champagne flutes available, the customer will have to wait until a clean flute is located, washed and delivered to the bar. Servers are never supposed to admit to a guest that the restaurant has run out of glasses. No one wants to explain to a paying customer that the expensive restaurant they are sitting in has no clean glasses available.

During a super busy, fast-paced, high-volume shift, shortcuts are taken on everything. Each person does whatever they have to do to keep up with the extremely nauseating, rapid flow. There is no exception when it comes to dishwashing. Glasses are run through the dishwasher as quickly as possible without being double-checked for crystal cleanliness. Worse than that, when the dishwasher is backed up, servers are sometimes forced to wash glasses by hand so the guests can keep drinking. The problem is, there is no restaurant protocol in place for handwashing dishes. This half-assed glass washing is why customers often find old lipstick on the rims of their supposedly clean glasses.

Servers don't get trained in washing dishes and certainly not by hand. There is no study guide, no class for this. There is no proper setup in the kitchen for it and no standard in place for how it should be done. So, in order to achieve this, the server must find three important things: some soap, a towel and some hot water. Because there is no protocol for this procedure, there is no dish soap, no clean towel and no hot water readily available to perform the task. If a server or bartender is handwashing glasses in the kitchen, how would she gather together these three important things? In cases like this, a server might use a rag—any rag she can find—perhaps coupled with a drop of soap from the hand wash dispenser, or even hand sanitizer. Or, perhaps no soap at all. And hot water? A good cold watery rub down may be all that poor glass receives.

Dishwashing by hand aside, handwashing itself is also a major concern among servers and kitchen staff. The washing of hands in this particular industry should be continuous and frequent, all the time, second-nature. Training manuals insist servers wash their hands. The little sign over the sink in the bathroom serves as a reminder too. However, many establishments do not enforce this requirement. Some don't bring it up at all.

Most times, servers walk right into work...and start working. Nobody regulates the handwashing to ensure all hands are clean before starting the shift. Servers may come to work and jump right into handling food, without ever going to the sink. Some servers may not wash their hands even once during a shift. Others, still, do not wash them frequently enough.

Most handwash sinks are located in the kitchen, directly next to or across from the dishpit. This is intentionally designed so that staff can conveniently wash their hands after dropping off dirty dishes. However, many servers drop off the dirty dishes, skip right past the sink, then move right back to handling new food and making new drinks. Even if they wanted to wash their hands, the handwash sink may not have soap, nor paper, ever. Some sinks don't even have working running water. Turn the knobs...and nothing. Before it reaches a table, a plate of food may have been touched by a half dozen sets of unwashed hands already. Without management enforcement of cleanliness in the workplace, sanitary matters can easily grow out of control and spill over into the dining room. It is surprising anyone can remain healthy in such an environment.

No one really does, actually. At some point, the filth and the germs collide and transform into some form of contagion that spreads quickly around the restaurant, making everyone sick with some disease or another. The bigger problem is that everybody continues to show up at work—illness in tow—like it's no big deal.

In the restaurant business, all staff go to work sick (Strutner, 2015). Everybody—dishwashers, cooks, bussers, servers, bartenders, managers too. Colds, influenza, headache, foot ache, diarrhea, back pain. Restaurant staff is often at work, battling all these ills simultaneously. An NPR survey on the matter confirms that over 50 percent of restaurant employees reported "always" or "frequently" going to work sick. An additional 38 percent admitted to doing this at least "sometimes" (Shallcross, 2015).

The staff does not go to work sick because they are so in love with their jobs. It is not okay to miss work in the restaurant industry—even for legitimate illness. With penalties waiting by management if you miss work, everybody goes to work sick. There is a great deal of pressure from restaurant management to either "show up" or "get fired." It's really that simple. Most of the staff have no health insurance and no access to immediate medical care anyway. With no speedy recovery in sight, they just keep showing up at work.

The high rate of working sick staff, multiplied by the low rate of handwashing, plus the imminent handling of food, equals a pretty good picture of how terribly unsanitary the entire restaurant environment can be. No wonder folks are paranoid about using plasticware and soaking silverware at the table. The ugly truth, however, is that soaking silverware is to no avail when half the staff is sick and/or the entire restaurant is filthy.

These are the nasty cruelties of the restaurant industry. Servers must work amidst filth that they cannot control, within constraints they cannot regulate, under management they cannot influence.

Yet they represent the face of the restaurant and bear the brunt of all the ills that take place there.

It's very simple. A serious restaurant can't half-ass its way through anything. A truly great restaurant will care so much about its customers that it will go above and beyond what is required to ensure guest satisfaction. They want customers to sit back, relax, and trust the restaurant to take care of them. They do not want their guests to worry or have concern about anything. With this great care in mind, they implement policies and procedures that ensure the restaurant is always clean—from top to bottom, from head to toe.

- The menu should be in excellent condition, free from food particles and grease stains.
- The entire table, everything on top and everything underneath, should be clean.
- The salt shakers and candleholders should be free of dust and particle debris.
- The flowers on the table should be real and fresh—not fake, wilted or dying.
- There should be no gum under the table and no trash and food crumbs on the floor.
- No unsightly trash and yucky debris in the cracks of the booth.
- Booth walls should be wiped clean.
- No uneven tables or wobbly chairs.
- Floors should be swept clean and freshly vacuumed.
- Walls and counters should be properly bathed.
- Shelves should be showered.
- All the bulbs in the light fixtures should be working.
- Plateware, glassware and silverware must be polished to a crystal clear, streak-free shine.

There will be no old lipstick stuck on a clean glass in a place like this. Everything will be clean. Even the servers' uniforms will be crisp, creased and wrinkle-free. Everything will be clean, including the restrooms and the kitchen, no matter what time you venture into them—both cleaned and restocked several times throughout the day like clockwork. Someone is assigned the task. The task is completed. Someone else follows behind to check that the assigned task is completed. Then, still another someone follows through to check the checker. This is necessary to ensure a restaurant gives its highest quality of service each and every single day. Cleanliness is not a game here.

Back of House

Basically, the back of house refers to the kitchen and all the kitchen staff. It consists of all the things and all the people beyond the dining room that the customer may never see. Amidst all the issues of management and cleanliness are the unthinkable truths which occur in the backs and bottoms of these ritzy establishments. As fancy and luxurious as they appear in the front, it is quite unimaginable how shitty things can be in the back.

Anthony Bourdain gives a very accurate description of the shameful shenanigans that go on in the back of house in his underworld tell-all *Kitchen Confidential* (2007). Marijuana is generally smoked in the backs of these facilities, sometimes unbeknownst to management, other times with management involved. Servers and cooks sell narcotics and other drugs to each other on the premises. Staff members get drunk and high at work all the time. It is a world of functioning addicts—from alcohol to cocaine, from pill-popping to crystal meth and everything in between.

The back of house is like that secret club with private members, hidden in the back of a restaurant, where folks sneak in for gambling and other suspicious activities. It is a drug-infested world of profanity, with an assorted array of transactions between employees for such things from drugs and sex to stolen meat and liquor, to fake identification cards and illegal documents. It can get wild. One might find a cook, smoking a cigarette in the kitchen while flipping the food on the grill—flipper in one hand, Newport in the other...flicking the cigarette ashes on the kitchen floor. It's more like a brothel than a kitchen back there.

The backyard madness is quite the contrast to the illusion of glitz and glamour people experience in the front. Some restaurants have no systems in place—no employee handbook, no training manual, no sexual harassment policy. In fact, the only system in place may be payroll, and even then, the accounting system (or the person in charge of it) may be suspect.

Most of these places are full of undocumented workers with kitchen staff who speak no English at all and can barely read the tickets to make the food. In fact, according to a 2008 report from the Pew Hispanic Center, undocumented workers account for at least 10 percent of the hospitality industry's workforce (Ralph, 2017). It is likely that even the 10 percent estimate is an underrepresentation as studies suggest over 20 percent of all cooks and 30 percent of all dishwashers are undocumented immigrants (Lempert, 2017).

The incredibly high employee turnover rates referred to earlier in the chapter, over 70 percent in the industry in 2015, push owners and managers to constantly hire under pressure or in a pinch, forcing them to fill vacant positions with anybody, regardless of their immigration status (Ralph, 2017). Many owners put the undocumented employees in place just to make it through the day. For them, it is easier to fill the spot and keep the business running and risk the penalties and fines, which may or may not surface at a later date.

The back of house cannot afford to be the jungle that it is. This level of craziness will ultimately affect everything in the kitchen, including the food. A walk into the cooler of a restaurant like this might reveal food, condiments and sauces with no date stamps or stickers. There inside may be random receptacles of various shapes and sizes all filled with unrecognizable substances—meaning, no one can identify the contents nor explain what the contents may have once been. Opening one of the containers might further reveal mold and bacteria and odor so foul that if inspectors popped up, they would shut the joint down on the spot. Some restaurants keep no track of when food was prepared, so the only way of knowing it's bad is by the smell of it, or when some customer sends the nastiness back to the kitchen. Then, everyone will know it was old. It happens.

As a matter of fact, it happens everywhere—not just in restaurant kitchens, but in stadium kitchens, museum kitchens, catering kitchens and all the kitchens of famous tourist attractions. Freshness is not guaranteed. Food is often far from fresh.

Imagine the following. There's a dinner at a local museum for 300 guests. It starts at 7 o'clock in the evening. The menu features an entrée of filet mignon and Chilean seabass. When was the filet and the seabass prepared? Well, to prepare food for 300 people, the cooking process has to start several hours before the event, perhaps even the day before. The cooks would prepare the steaks and the fish well in advance, store them in a cooler, then reheat the food before the event. The time between when the food is prepared and when the food is served can be quite lengthy. A lot can happen to the food during that waiting time.

If the food must be transported from an off-site kitchen to the actual event venue, then the food has to be moved from the cooler to a truck and driven there. The trucks are not always refrigerated.

So, the food may ride in a sweltering hot truck, only to then be removed and set in an unrefrigerated room for several hours. The steak may be tainted, and the seafood may be spoiled...yet they will be still plated and served.

The truth is that most of these companies suffer gravely from inefficiency and disorganization. When assigned with the task of facilitating an event for a several hundred people, these places transform into production plants. The food is plated in a human assembly line, reminiscent of an automobile factory making thousands of cars. Their primary goal is to produce 300 identical plates. No one cares that the fish is fishy or that the steak is cold. The goal is to get the food out on the table.

Even at sports arenas, freshness can be seriously compromised. Staff at these facilities must implement painstaking measures to ensure food is served at the correct temperature and thrown out after sitting for a certain amount of time. However, the issue of constantly revolving staff members at each food station creates a significant problem. At each game, there is new staff and temporary event staff. Many of the workers have only learned how to work the station that same day, shortly before the gates open, and they do not have enough longevity in the position to proactively care about the proper food regulations. Freshness becomes a happenstance or just a mere possibility.

Dystopia of Discrimination

Racism and sexism still run quite rampant in possibly every facet of American culture. The restaurant business is no exception. Again, because the restaurant industry operates under its own set of laws, acts of racism and sexism occur more frequently and continuously go unchecked. Unlike the passive-aggressive discrimination in conventional corporate America, the discriminative atmosphere in the restaurant industry is outright and wretched. There is no discretion, no yellow tape. There are no filters. Racism and sexism smack the staff right in the face on a daily basis. Language most employees would be instantly terminated for, restaurant staff embellishes and enunciates at the tops of their lungs. Racist and sexist remarks for which people lose their entire careers over are thrown back and forth through the kitchen like a football, while spectators laugh and cheer and go right back to work.

Everybody is unfazed by all the slander and slurs, the disrespectful jokes. Oddly, those who can dish it and take it best are highly rewarded with some false sense of restaurant cred. Anthony Bourdain painstakingly describes the essence of this brutal exchange in *Kitchen Confidential* (2007). In the kitchen, there is so much preoccupation with touching, grabbing, poking and/or squeezing someone's ass that it poses itself as a sexual rite of passage for the servers and cooks. Just like athletes, restaurant staff are expected to embrace the pain, to play through the pain and become tougher. Those who can endure this kitchen torture, then retaliate with the appropriate amount of pain in kind can earn the worship of kings while at work. However, once the offensive words begin to fly, it is only a matter of time before somebody makes a racist or sexist remark.

Working in the restaurant industry in the state of Georgia, one is privy and subject to a hefty share of racist situations. Although Atlanta, its capital city, is a politically blue city, it is completely landlocked within an all red state. Amidst all the notions of liberty and freedom in Atlanta, the city still suffers from old, antiquated ideals and people who hold steadfast to them. So as much as black folks sport a wide array of natural hairstyles—afros, dreadlocks, cornrows, braids—there are still people who prefer the black folks they hire conform to the norms of the Old White South. In order to work in the affluent neighborhoods, in restaurants where people spend lots of money, black folks must shave it, gel it down or smooth it back to make both management and guests feel comfortable. Blacks must become non-threatening in every way to work there.

This is what management is looking for in new applicants—polish. When they claim they want employees who are *polished*, it is restaurant code for black folks who are willing to shave it up, gel it down and smooth it back. A bald head, a nice perm, a good weave—no visual kinks and coils to remind anyone of real blackness. They want applicants who slick themselves down. Afros, dreadlocks, cornrows and braids are unwelcomed in these pretentious places. Out of the daily pool of black folks who might stop by one of these restaurants to apply in person, it would be easy to predict who would get hired and who would not—all based on the person's skin complexion and the person's hair texture and its degree of nappiness.

Staff promotions work the same way. As sad as it is to admit, some of the high-end restaurants promote black servers based on skin complexion and hair type. The way they go about doing this is obvious and indiscreet. Black men who are bald are coveted because they are non-threatening to the establishment and, thus, easily promoted. Black females with lighter skin complexions and/or wavy hair texture, or a good weave, can be promoted within weeks into positions others have been waiting for years to fill.

Restaurants have their fair share of sexism as well. There are so-called "upscale" chains that require the female servers to wear a uniform consisting of a short-sleeved V-neck t-shirt, a miniskirt, fishnet stockings and high-heeled leather boots. Meanwhile, the male servers wear the standard, professional, full server uniform with a long-sleeved button-down dress shirt, dress slacks and a necktie. How is a restaurant full of male managers supposed to effectively manage a group of females wearing miniskirts and fishnets all night? What happens when a shapely server in a miniskirt, fishnet stockings and high-heeled leather boots bends over to pick up a spoon? Needless to say, in an environment with such a dress code, the male managers and male cooks (and male customers too) easily become sexual deviants and sexual vultures—constantly preying on the half-naked female staff.

Many male managers treat their female employees like animal prey rather than like human beings. Hence, a restaurant run by all male management is never good for staff. Men in management manage with their penises. Whether they realize it or not, they are easily manipulated by female employees. The big breasts and backsides of women make them uncomfortable and unprofessional. They cannot separate work from play, nor distinguish ass from apron. Because of this, they show favoritism towards some female employees while believing they are hiding it from the others. Many of them offer hugs where handshakes should be, and some hugs last way too long. Male managers get fired all the time for having sexual relations with the female staff.

At Bootcamp Restaurant, the male owner of the chain demanded that the female servers wear lipstick. He would have the general manager—a female—bring in a bag of tubes in a variety of colors—mostly bright red—for the servers to choose from. Each female server had to choose at least one tube of lipstick from the bag, or be fired—it was not optional. The servers were monitored, both in person and by remote video, to ensure they were wearing lipstick every day.

Apparently, the owner already knew what researchers have tested and proven. Male customers are more attracted to red lipstick—the color being associated with estrogen levels and sexual arousal (Fishbein, 2012). In fact, female servers who wear red lipstick even get tipped more. Researchers from the Université de Bretagne-Sud "studied seven waitresses who served 447 customers in three restaurants in France, discovering that those who wore red lipstick earned up to 50 percent more in tips...," (Fishbein, 2012). "Male patrons gave tips more frequently to waitresses wearing red lipstick than to other waitresses, and when they tipped, they gave more," (Parry, 2012). This owner had already made the connection between red lipstick and its power to draw more money from his wealthy male clientele. He was now imposing this sexist logic on his female staff.

Forcing female employees to wear lipstick is a textbook example of how blatant passive sexism can be. In most of these restaurants, racism and sexism exist simultaneously. It is not uncommon for staff, especially women, to endure the stress of both at the same time.

The Predator's Playground

Of course, when dealing with staff who regularly poke and prod each other's private parts, there will ultimately be legal consequences and repercussions. This is still America—land of the lawsuit. When he grew tired of his colleague poking him in the ass, Chef Anthony Bourdain simply caught his offender on the next try and drove a meat fork through his knuckles (Bourdain, 2007). If everyone in the restaurant handled sexual harassment this way, potentially half of the staff would be working in bandages.

Sexual harassment is so pervasive in this industry that most cases go unreported. Both women and men suffer from repeated bouts of inappropriate behavior. Because it happens so frequently, victims try to toughen up, then find themselves putting up with the harassment in order to keep their jobs. Although over 70 percent of servers are women (ROCUnited.org), they still work in a male-dominated industry. Men hold most, if not all, of the key positions of power. A lot of the misconduct towards women—from both staff and customers—is swept under the rug by the men in charge. Yet still, even as most cases go unreported, the restaurant industry ranks highest—meaning, number one—in sexual harassment cases (Angyal, 2015).

> *Of all the sexual harassment claims that the Equal Employment Opportunity Commission receives every year, fully 37 percent of them come from one place: the restaurant industry. That makes the restaurant industry the largest source of sexual harassment claims to the EEOC in the nation – and that's before you account for the fact that sexual harassment is underreported* (Angyal, 2015).

Even though the percentage of women in the country who actually work in the industry is small, well under 10 percent, they account for a whopping 37 percent of all reported sexual harassment cases.

> *And even though just seven percent of American women work in the restaurant industry, a review of EEOC charge data by the Restaurant Opportunities Center (ROC) United over an eleven-month period in 2011 found that nearly 37 percent of EEOC sexual harassment charges came from women in the restaurant industry* (EEOC, 2015).

The combination of working in close quarters with the requirement for continuous bending over, plus the rights of free speech, added to the propensity for sexual deviance, including, but not limited to, sexual relations between co-workers, compounded by managers sleeping with staff members intensifies the harassment issue. All these variables together make the line between acceptance and offense very blurry.

Sexual harassment is only harassment when it is unsolicited, unwanted.

> *Although the law doesn't prohibit simple teasing, offhand comments, or isolated incidents that are not very serious, harassment is illegal when it is so frequent or severe that it creates a hostile or offensive work environment or when it results in an*

> *adverse employment decision (such as the victim being fired or demoted)* (EEOC.gov).

Part of the problem in the restaurant industry is: some of the staff actually like the touching, the sexual games, the boyhood-like wrestling, the rank rough-housing and curious genital horseplay. There is a superfine line between the "simple teasing" and "offhand comments" which are legally ignored and the true harassment that is considered illegal. In fact, it is the teasing, the comments and the "isolated incidents" that lead to the actual, very real hostile environment which becomes sexual harassment. If the teasing and offhand comments are allowed, harassment is almost inevitable. It is best to create an environment where professionalism is priority and to simply eliminate the teasing and comments altogether.

Measures must be put into place to lessen the potential for harassment. Strict adherence of the laws should be enforced and executed at all times. This is the best way to keep staff protected and safe. This is the only way to keep a restaurant from being drenched in EEOC paperwork and running in and out of court.

ABOUT SERVERS

FALLACY VS. FACT

Servers and similar positions of service are not valued in American society. The antebellum attitudes of yesterday still prevail regarding service work. These types of jobs are associated with the poor and uneducated--those citizens in the population who are poverty-stricken and cannot afford the type of education that leads to a valuable career. Valuable careers are generally defined as those which reflect large income, salaried pay, and medical benefits. They are esteemed jobs, also service-oriented, yet because they are respected by society, these jobs (doctors, lawyers, bankers, etc.) are revered as rewarding and respectable. These are among the careers many Americans traditionally hope to see their children strive toward.

Serving food is not rocket science. A job whereby a person is merely dropping off plates to tables and refilling water glasses does not appear to require a skillset level high enough to warrant respect from the collective population. In our modern world of reality television, the position of cook, which, with the utmost respect we now utter as "Chef," is the only service position in the food industry that has been elevated to a level of prestige and esteem. The rest of the industry staff are simply viewed by the rest of the world as lost, low-lifes and losers—unfit for the more appropriate career job.

On the contrary, waiting tables requires a level of high-skilled multi-tasking that most people could never successfully achieve. Serving food and drink is not so simple as dropping off plates and refilling water. It is highly complicated, extremely demanding work. Despite the pressure they endure in their corporate positions, most doctors, lawyers and bankers would not last 30 minutes waiting tables in a restaurant. The dedication and attention necessary to attend to the needs of many tables at once requires a memory level and a unique skillset only a small segment of the population is likely able to sustain.

To be able to suggest to a stranger the perfect meal he should eat requires knowledge of the chemistry of available flavors as well as the ability to take this knowledge and pair it with the consumption personality of the diner. To carry food and deliver beverages for several hours a day, all while maintaining a crisp, clean, professional appearance requires charisma and grace. To work while walking on throbbing feet and standing on aching muscles requires tolerance and discipline. In essence, servers are like food and beverage counselors who must understand both food and people in order to help people make food choices that will facilitate a happy dining experience. This is no small task.

All in all, in light of everything known about what happens in restaurants, the server is the one who works amidst the disgust and filth, the profanity and disrespect, the sexism and racism, and still delivers star service to the unknowing customer who just wants to have a nice meal and a good time. All of this is accomplished while maintaining calm in the face of chaos, approaching each table brand new without carrying the issues from one table over to the next one. With both sides of the brain dominating simultaneously, while also attempting to filter out the daily wretchedness, the server is both a brilliant genius and a certifiable nutcase the entire time he or she is working.

First off, everything hurts. The head aches from all the bullshit. The arms ache from carrying heavy plates and trays. The back aches from the constant bending and lifting of 30-pound boxes. The feet ache from walking over 20,000 steps a day, often accumulated in a matter of a few hours. The average server walks approximately 10 miles per day. "A study by weight loss company Jenny Craig found that waiters take 23,000 steps a day, more than double the recommended 10,000 steps a day to keep fit," (Hernandez, 2012). While at work, on a regular shift between 6 to 8 hours, a server can walk between 7 to 12 miles around a restaurant.

Just imagine. If a waiter walks 10 miles inside a restaurant, this feat is accomplished by walking around in circles, up and down, back and forth through the aisles of an often dimly lit square box—like a laboratory rat in a maze. They wear through shoes like pubescent teenage boys—always needing a new pair every few months. Because of all this walking, waiters are the fittest of workers by trade (Westcott, 2012). They walk more than nurses, teachers and farmers (Hernandez, 2012). However, because of all this walking, they may also be the most likely to suffer long term, serious feet problems. What's worse is the fact that, as servers burn more calories than they consume, all this walking is usually conducted on a consistently empty stomach. This is why waiters magically appear from nowhere and scramble like roaches to any plate of food that is up for grabs in the kitchen. A full plate of french fries can disappear in the literal blink of an eye. All the walking creates a sense of true starvation.

Servers are smart. They must retain a great deal of information regarding food and beverages. It is not so simple as merely memorizing a menu. Servers must know the ingredients of all the foods on the menu, including detailed ingredients of condiments and sauces, and be able to communicate all this in an impressive spiel to customers who have no clue what they want. They must understand a variety of allergies, including shellfish, tree nuts, wheat gluten, soy, citrus and everything else to ensure customer safety and satisfaction. They must know which foods a customer can and cannot enjoy, so as to avoid allergic reactions from the customers they serve, lest someone from one of their tables ends up leaving in an ambulance...it happens. Avoiding the paramedics means understanding the ingredients of every item, all the way down to every herb, every oil, every type of juice, as well as each and all seasonings used to prepare every dish. This feat, in and of itself, is enormous. As proof, new servers in training at almost every fine dining restaurant carry around a big, fat, 3-inch, 5-pound binder full of superfluous food and beverage descriptions from which they have studied for weeks as if trying to pass the bar for a legal career.

Servers have extensive knowledge about wine and alcohol from all over the world. They know the origins and history of all the wine and alcohol. Servers have to study and be thoroughly tested on alcoholic beverages and cocktails. They know beer. They know bubbles. They become experts on wine varietals and vintage and can elaborate on the crucial differences between whiskey and bourbon. They are equipped with the ability to recommend drinks to people they have just met and remember drinks people enjoy whom they've only met once. Even greater, servers (just like bartenders) are responsible for the alcohol they serve to their customers. Servers are trained to gauge the characteristics of each customer based on behavior, size, gender and several other important factors. Then, servers must weigh these variables to determine the possibility of serving more alcohol to that customer. It is illegal to serve alcohol to an already visibly intoxicated person (Alcohol.org, 2020).

Not only are servers and bartenders responsible for serving alcohol to intoxicated guests, they can be sued for liability and damages if a guest consumes too much alcohol and behaves irresponsibly—whether they leave the restaurant on wheels or on foot (National Conference of State Legislatures, 2013). At least 30 states have adopted some measure of these "dram shop" laws. Dram shop civil liability laws hold the person selling the alcohol responsible—not just the drinker—for any damage that happens by that drinker after that drinker leaves the facility in a drunken state. Over half the states in our country hold an equal measure of liability on both the buyer and the seller (NCSL, 2013). One can easily end up in court and/or in jail for selling alcohol to an already-intoxicated individual. This is a pretty serious consequence for something seemingly as simple as dropping off food and drink.

Servers have to work well with guests, managers, cooks, hosts and other servers simultaneously. This requires an enormous amount of communication, the balancing of multiple tasks and working with varied attitudes and diverse personalities. Servers must be multi-faceted communicators with the ability to "read" people, to be able to gauge the different moods and attitudes of both colleagues and strangers. Many servers have worked extensively as waitstaff, having served in various positions at many different restaurants over a period of time. This equips them with the knowledge and ability to understand and cope with various management structures and diverse management personalities and training techniques. Because of this, some servers are better-qualified to manage the restaurants they work in than the actual managers themselves, but still must work under the supervision of often unqualified, inefficient or failing management.

Servers, specifically servers working in a fine dining atmosphere, are far from weak and uneducated. On the contrary, these servers are usually highly intelligent, extremely knowledgeable, articulate and proficient. They are well-rounded and world-travelled. They are physically fit and visually beautiful. On any random fine dining roster will be a diverse group of brilliant artists and intellectuals--students paying their own way through school, artists saving money to support their dreams, single mothers raising their children and paying their bills. These people know the ins and outs of the business like the backs of their hands. They know what and what not to order, what's nasty, what's fresh or not, what's not worth the price. They know how to ring in free things or discounted items. They know the low-down, and they have the hook-up. It would be wise to treat them well.

Servers are extremely valuable to the restaurant industry and to the dining experience. They are an absolute necessity. Servers are the face of the restaurant. The server is the person of whom the guest will ask almost all questions. Servers have the answer. Servers often offer the first impression of the experience to the guest, and the server's name and face is what will be remembered when the guest reminisces on the experience and considers a return visit to the establishment.

Contrary to societal standards, servers and similar positions of service have tremendous value in the workplace. The way people judge and dismiss them is unacceptable. They are human beings with parents and children and families. They are brothers and sisters and have aunts and uncles just like everyone else. They deserve the same reverence a doctor, lawyer or banker would receive while providing the respective services they provide at work. The same is true of bartenders, bussers, valet attendants, bellhops, janitors, housekeepers, rideshare drivers and all the positions which have been historically shameful to hold because of society's insistence on upholding classism and oppression. It is not cool to treat any person in a negative way or view any person in a negative light because of the amount of his pay.

THE TAO OF TIPPING

The Unspoken Pact

By sitting down at a restaurant table, the guest makes a silent mutual pact with the server. There is an unspoken agreement that they will both take care of each other. The server will provide friendly service by answering questions with a pleasant demeanor and offering suggestions that will ensure an awesome experience. The server goes the extra mile for the delight of the guest and caters to the guest to make sure the guest wants for nothing. The guest returns the kindness with a grateful attitude and a responsible tip. It is an honest human exchange of the most basic kind—reciprocity.

Problems arise when one of these two does not fulfill his end of this agreement. The server, because he is at work, is most likely to carry out all his duties. The issue at hand, however, is that the guest is not obligated to do so. When the guest does not fulfill his end of this unwritten agreement, an infraction occurs. A law is broken.

A most critical question is: Where did this agreement come from?

Before the Civil War, white landowners were able to legally exploit their slaves as property and profit from the free labor the slaves provided. After the Civil War, however, when slavery was legally abolished, these same business owners scrambled to create new ways to still gain profit from free labor (Jayaraman, 2016). They wanted the newly freed slaves to continue to work for them without paying them anything—slavery still but with a new name.

This was the essence of the notion behind sharecropping. White landowners, now former slaveowners because of the war, needed the slaves to continue to work the land. They contracted with their former slaves, convincing them that they could stay and toil the land in exchange for a share of the crop (Giesen, 2007). Though the contracts varied from county to county, most of them were set up as predatory credit systems, whereby black sharecroppers only received a small fraction of the crop they produced. The small profit from those crops was then used to pay back what they owed to white landowners for such expenses as rent, food, equipment and supplies (Giesen, 2007). Many of the newly freed blacks hoped they would eventually gain ownership of land for themselves. They stayed and worked the land in agreement with their former masters, only to discover they were charged so much for these necessary expenses with such little profit, they would be forever indebted to white landowners and never able to leave (Giesen, 2007).

The American tipping system, also instituted after the Civil War, is akin to the sharecropping system. They were both adopted by white American land and business owners to manipulate free men and women into providing labor without compensation. The tipping system, however, allowed the black workers who serve white patrons to make money from the patrons themselves, who tipped them for their service. This allowed the black tipped workers to afford some measure of halfway decent life, while allowing the white patrons to reinforce their feelings of superiority over the black workers...while still allowing the white business owners to profit without paying the free black workers from their own pockets ((Jayaraman, 2016).

Hence, a new relationship was forged between the free black workers and the dining public—an unwritten, unspoken reciprocity. For a hundred years, this practice was developed through several generations of cultural behavior strictly between the two—black workers and white patrons. Although the agreement was between these two, it was enforced by the business owner who, without fronting a dime to the worker, still monitored and policed the exchange. Of course, the agreement is completely flawed, but it is the agreement, nonetheless.

This agreement has evolved only slightly over time, based on how times have changed. The times have changed because the workers and patrons have changed. Whereas before, it was only a situation of blacks serving whites, today both the worker and the patron can be black or white or of any race or color. As a result, the old school tipping agreement is blurred and shrouded in confusion.

Today, the non-white patrons who dine out have no investment in any historical agreement with the workers. Because they are not white people, the unwritten agreement has no historical context for them. Generally, they don't tip to feel superior over the worker. They tip because they live in America and that's what Americans do. They tip because it is a societal norm. Because American restaurant owners have sustained the policy of not paying their workers for over 150 years, the unspoken pact is still in place between the workers and the patrons. Because the racial demographics of the patron have changed, so has the tipping point. However, black people seem to be the only segment of society who simply refuse to honor the pact. The reason why is directly related to their historical connection to the origins of the agreement.

Serving white folks is an integral part of black history. Black folks have been cooking and cleaning and serving white folks for hundreds of years. When it comes to this historical agreement, black people are somewhat psychologically dysfunctional. The black patron is new. They are historically on the worker side, not the patron side—tip receivers, not tip givers. They recognize the disparity in the pay from the business owner, and they know inherently that the business owner should be the one to suffer the expense of paying workers. Their refusal to honor the tipping system is a protest to the tipping system, the business owner, and the very idea of capitalism itself.

There is a major problem with this protest. While black folks are protesting the tipping system, they are still psychologically bound to the historical superiority complex that they adopted from the white patrons of the past. As patrons, they expect to be catered to with excellent service, but they refuse to reciprocate with the healthy attitude and the proper tip. So black folks violate the unspoken pact often, and they continuously upset the restaurant business status quo. Now that they are on the patron side of the restaurant equation, they must come to grips with the established agreement. Meanwhile, they are hurting the workers in the process, most of whom are their own kind. The exact opposite should be the case. Knowing that their own people are the ones working in these positions and tolerating this industry, there should be more understanding and love toward the worker. It's a twisted narrative.

Two Thirteen

So...during the period of reconstruction following the Civil War, the system of tipping was popularized to disparage blacks. Today, the same system is still in place, hurting people of all colors who must work within it. Whereas before the workers were paid solely based on tips, today they still work solely based on tips. This twisted tipping practice from the 19th century, post-Civil War era is the same abusive system of 21st century America today. It is fundamentally the same system from 150 years ago.

Most servers and other tipped restaurant employees across the country make approximately two dollars per hour base pay salary. To be exact, the Federal Labor Standards Act dictates that all states adhere to the minimum wage standard for tipped employees, which is $2.13 per hour (United States Department of Labor, 2017).

There are some exceptional states, such as California and Nevada, which require employers to pay tipped employees the full state minimum wage before tips, which can be well over $7.00 per hour before tips (USDOL, 2017). The rest, however, hover slightly above or precisely target the $2.13 per hour. This means that a server working 40 hours a week will make about $80.00 each week for base pay. This pay structure implies that workers will take home the base pay, *plus* the additional money earned from tips. However, no one ever sees this money. The $2.13 per hour is an invisible ghost.

No different than any other job whereby a worker makes a certain salary and a percentage of the wages are taken by taxes, the tipped income a server earns during a 40-hour work week is subject to be taxed. So, for example, if a server earns $600 per week in tips and owes $100 in taxes, the $80 she earned from the $2.13 base pay will be taken away by the IRS. It will be automatically deducted through the company's accounting process. Since the $80.00 only covers *some* of the taxes, not all of them, the remaining $20 that the server owes in taxes for that week must be paid to the IRS directly out-of-pocket from the server. The server is responsible for reporting her annual income to the IRS and paying them the rest of what is owed. This means that any and all money a server takes home must come from somewhere else—from somewhere else other than the $2.13 per hour. It means the server's pay is entirely dependent upon the tips they receive.

To make tipping matters even worse, before the taxes are taken, many restaurants require servers to "tip-out" all server support staff—the hosts, the food runners, the bussers, the server assistants, the bartenders, the barbacks. All these positions similarly receive low hourly pay which must be supplemented by the tips from the servers. After the tips are tallied at the end of each shift, a percentage of the tips is automatically deducted from each server and divvied up among the support staff. Even before the taxes are confiscated by the IRS, a significant portion of a server's tips have already been repossessed by management.

Tip-out systems and percentages vary. In some restaurants, the tip-out is a percentage of a server's tips and can be as high as 40 percent (Restaurant Tip Laws, 2017). Using an example with simple mathematics, this means that if a server makes $100 on a shift, they must first tip-out $30 dollars to support staff, leaving them with $70 before taxes. Obviously, the less money the server makes, the less money there is to tip-out the support staff. When the server does not receive the proper tips, it affects the entire staff.

Other restaurants base the tip-out amount on a percentage of a server's sales, taking as much as 5 percent or more of total food and beverage sales. For example, a server might sell $1000 worth of food and beverages on a shift. The required tip-out is 5 percent of this number, meaning they must tip-out $50. Well, based on the expectation and calculation of earning 20 percent in tips, the server should have earned close to $200 for $1000 worth of food and drink. At a tip-out of 5 percent of sales, the server would tip-out $50, leaving $150 to take home. But here's where everything gets really tricky and why the tips are so important. The server must tip-out the 5 percent ($50) regardless of how much he makes in tips. If he were to earn less than 20 percent in tips...say 15 percent in tips, he would earn $150 in tips and tip-out $50 and have $100 left. But say there were two or three tables that undertipped him or left him no tip at all, and all he made in tips that shift was $100. He would still be required to tip-out $50 based on the $1000 worth of sales. He would make $50 in tips for the entire shift—for 7 or more hours of labor.

This is why there is so much fuss about the 20 percent tip. When servers don't get tipped properly, it directly affects either the server and all the support staff in the restaurant. If the server does not get paid, these folks don't get paid either.

It is interesting how the businesses in this industry continue to discover new ways to pay their workers from pockets other than their own, to work people without actually paying them. The tip-out system is merely an extension of the tipping system, whereby the patrons pay the wages of the servers, then the servers pay the wages of the support staff. Meanwhile, the company profits while its employees suffer.

Emily Post's *Etiquette* suggests that the main issue of America's tipping dilemma lies within this $2.00 per hour salary. Because waitstaff are paid less than minimum wage, tipping becomes a requirement, a duty of the patron. The public diner becomes responsible for not just the tip, but for the very income of the waitstaff. Meaning, the tip *is* the income. And if the tip is the income, then it is no longer a tip, it is simply income. In essence, the American public is providing the income to tipped employees, and they are tipping out of public obligation. As long as diners are forced to financially supplement this disparity, tipping can never be used to reflect the quality of service received by the patron (Post, 2011). The line between who deserves what and who gets how much is blurred beyond distinction. Do you tip because you liked the service, or do you tip because you are supposed to? According to Post (2011), tipping has traditionally been used primarily to reflect how patrons felt about the service they received. This privilege has been destroyed by the requirement to tip all waitstaff based on the economic fact they receive only $2.00 per hour.

Post may be correct, but despite her argument, there are many diners who understand very little about how much servers get paid, and they *do* tip strictly according to the measure of service they receive. This does not uncomplicate the issue, however. Tipping, whether it be for quality of service or out of obligation, is a convoluted subject matter. Customers can tip—or not tip—for any one of a million different absurd or justifiable reasons. Fact is, it does not matter *why* a customer is tipping because the entire tipping system itself is a creation for oppression and subjugation, and it only leaves room for confusion, judgement, irregularity, unfairness, discrimination and inequality toward the workers involved.

Fear, Food and Money

If the art of tipping is a learned or adapted behavior, then where do black folks learn it from? Gerry Fernandez of the Multicultural Foodservice and Hospitality Alliance puts it this way,

> *Tipping behavior has to be looked at in its totality. We have to look at it for its cultural elements, for the institutionalized racism that exists in this industry, and then education. How do people learn about tipping? If you don't go, you don't know...If that is not learned behavior at home, then how can you expect any particular group to understand what the norm is around tipping?* (Dublanica, 2010)

Many times, black folks truly appreciate remarkable service. They will even say so. They will ask for a manager so that they can compliment the server. They will hunt the server down in the restaurant to hand them a cash tip, rather than risk leaving it on the table. They will write a 'thank you' note for you on the merchant receipt, "you were wonderful," "best service ever," "you rock," etc. They make it painfully obvious that they thought they were doing something special on your behalf. Then they still proceed to leave a substandard tip.

This is the proof that, many times, black diners do mean well. They do value great service and indeed strive to do the right thing. They simply have no idea that their tip offering is not up to par. They are clueless about what it means to do something special because they have yet to understand what the standard baseline is. Basically, they can't leave an extra nice tip if they don't know the difference between a bad tip and a good tip.

Although all the nice reviews from customers are welcomed and appreciated, they do substitute nor take the place of a proper tip. And frankly, the offering of such warm remarks and seemingly genuine appreciation only leave a poor server completely discombobulated when accompanied by a poor tip. A 'thank you' note attached to a $5 tip on a $100 tab never leaves a server with a feeling of appreciation. Instead, it leaves them with a sense of confusion, and it adds confirmation to the culture bias that already exists.

Many black folks have a dysfunctional relationship with money. This perception, this disconnection was passed down through struggling generations of ancestors who believed money to be a finite concept—a belief that there is only so much to go around. Money was for survival and rarely used for happy experiences and spontaneous joy. With such an attitude toward money, it is difficult for many black folks to enjoy a fine dining experience without some sort of worrisome impulse to reduce the bill in some way. It is even more difficult to fathom leaving $30 or $40 for a tip, regardless of how much the bill total is. Four people at a fine dining establishment can easily rack up a bill of $200 or more by ordering appetizers, entrees and cocktails. A bill this size, warranting a proper 20 percent tip, would be $40 easily. Others who dine out understand this and oblige accordingly. Black folks, however, have an extremely difficult time wrapping their heads around leaving a tip so large. It is hard to let the money go.

This fact particularly stands true when considering that black folks do not consider the tip as a viable part of the meal. They are mostly concerned with the food they ate and only committed to paying for that. Because the tip is listed as an added-on expense, it is considered "extra," which can easily translate into a perception of something unnecessary. The tip is viewed as money given away for free. The food they are obligated to pay for, the tip not so much. So...sometimes the tip is not based on some pre-suggested percentage, but rather how much that person feels comfortable with spending the money and letting it go. This level of comfort trumps everything. It takes precedence over server expectations and societal norms that demand 20 percent.

Many restaurants offer suggestions for the proper amount to tip, usually at the bottom of the receipt. The suggested tip amount printed on the receipt is there to help guide the diner regarding what tip amount is appropriate. Black folks ignore the tip suggestion on the receipt and tip whatever amount they choose, based on the dollar amount they feel comfortable with.

Consider the case whereby a black patron leaves a $10 tip when the server may have been expecting $20. The tip may be subpar according to the tipping system, but to the black patron, the tip is sufficient. This is because, to most black folks, a $10 tip is a lot of money to offer someone without obligation. From the general black perspective, $10 is still a lot of money. So, to offer 10 bucks as a tip, as an extra gesture on top of what is actually owed, feels like a nice offering. Here lies the essence of the tipping disconnection between black patrons and those who serve them. It is a cultural matter of economic perspective.

KASSONDRA ROCKSWELL

The Ten Buck Round Up

In the black community, the number 10 and the 10-dollar bill are of significance. Ten is a "go to" number for everyday dealings and transactions. It is the amount of money one might loan a friend. It is the standard cover fee to enter a club. It is the amount of money one might spend on a decent meal or pay for gas on pump two.

Ten is a nice and easy, round, whole number—easy to divide, easy to multiply. In the restaurant, black folks often apply the same methodology of the number 10 when calculating a tip.

For instance, a party of black folks spend $64.50 on a meal. The person paying the bill leaves a total of $70.00, tipping the server $5.50. $5.50 is an inadequate tip for a $65 bill. In actuality, at the rate of 20%, $5.50 is less than half of what the server deserves. Nevertheless, black people often calculate their tips this way. They automatically round up to the next whole dollar, in the tens place. If the bill is $64, they leave exactly $70. If the bill is $73, they leave $80. If the bill is $92, they leave $100. What is the justification for this round-off? Could it be connected to a cultural preoccupation of the number 10 and the 10-dollar bill?

If the bill happens to be an inconvenient number like $69.25 or $78.50—where the total does not allow the tipper to simply round up to the nearest ten, then the tip is simply either $5 or $10. Once the bill approaches or passes the vicinity of $100, black folks will drop a $10 bill and leave. These are very real, specific patterns of gratuity that many black people display in the exact same way under the same circumstances.

Truth is, most black folks are extremely uncomfortable tipping over $10, no matter how high they run up a bill. It's the "Ten on Two" syndrome—put $10 on Pump 2, no matter the price of gasoline...put $10 on Table 2, no matter the price of the bill. This gesture is not to intentionally offend servers. Again, it is a cultural matter of economic perspective. To offer an entire $10 is at most times with the best intentions.

Other times, however, intentions may not be so great. There are times when black folks leave no tip whatsoever. Amazingly still, others will go so far as to pay cash for the bill and be short on the money without leaving the proper total of the bill. It is difficult to make any excuses for such behavior. The problem is, those folks with good intentions and those with not-so-good intentions get thrown into the same pot, when there are definite distinctions between the two. Though their tips may be deemed small, some black folks mean well in their offering, while others simply don't care at all.

The problem is, regardless of intention, to the server, a short tip is insufficient to show gratitude for great service received from caring, attentive, efficient waitstaff. To them, it is insulting and unpleasantly redundant. In almost every case, when a guest leaves a tip lower than one of the suggested amounts, meaning, lower than 15 percent, it is almost always a black person or black party.

Black folks' tipping perspective may be also affected by the way they worship. Christian black folks acquired an early understanding of giving from experience with the black church, within which also lies an important reference to the number ten. While over 80 percent of black folks are Christians (Pew Research Center, 2015), the effects of Christian teachings regarding giving and money are far-reaching.

Tithing, the Christian law that governs how much one should give of his personal wealth to God, only requires members to give 10 percent to the church. If the Lord only asks for 10 percent, how dare some measly, plate-totin' server demand more than that.

However, tithing requires 10 percent of one's entire income, whereas tipping is only a percentage of one's meal. This 10 percent understanding of giving is subconscious in the mentality of black folks, perhaps even among those who do not, or who no longer, consider themselves Christians. Somehow, the automatic comparison of tipping to tithing has brought about mass confusion among Christian black folks who dine out. Many black folks use the 10 percent tithe as an excuse to leave an inadequate tip.

It is often these "holier than thou" type of black folks who frequent restaurants and exhibit the least holy behavior. Many of them go directly from church, straight to the restaurant—just having praised the Lord, dressed up in Sunday's best—and act like agents of the devil. They are disrespectful, demanding, rude, mistrustful, entitled, pilfering, fearful and withholding—none of the characteristics of Jesus Christ, the Lord they have just glorified in worship and praise.

WHAT WOULD JESUS TIP?

In January 2013, a party of black folks dined at an Applebee's restaurant in suburban St. Louis, Missouri after some type of church service. The party consisted of 10 guests, including five children. After finishing the meal, they requested split checks. According to the story, which aired on major television networks, including MSNBC, CNN, ABC and FOX, one of the guests had an issue with the bill (Erb, 2013).

Apparently, the woman did not appreciate the automatic gratuity which was standard for parties of eight or more at the Applebee's location. Her bill was a total of $34.93. The 18 percent automatic gratuity added $6.29 to the bill. The unhappy woman crossed out the automatic gratuity and signed "Pastor" next to the crossout. Next to it, she wrote a very interesting note to the server on the receipt.

> "I give God 10 percent, why should you get 18"

The server who served the party then showed the receipt to another server, Chelsea Welch. Ms. Welch thought that the comment was so ridiculous that she took a picture of it and posted it to a social media website. The posting of the photo went viral with thousands of viewers, comments and postings, so much so that it became headline news for major television networks (Dolak, 2013).

After the pastor found out about the post and how big it had blown up, she demanded Applebee's fire Chelsea Welch, the server who served them, as well as everyone on duty in the restaurant for embarrassing her. Applebee's made a statement regarding the matter in favor of the guest. Of course, Ms. Welch lost her job.

The pastor, Prophetess Alois Bell, apparently fell under some scrutiny by her own community and her own congregation for being a "hypocritical pastor." She obviously felt even more embarrassed from being chastised by the church than she claimed she felt at the restaurant. After calling the restaurant and demanding everyone be terminated, Prophetess Bell later admitted in a CNN interview that her actions had been "stupid," citing a "lapse in judgment." Ms. Bell also admitted that she wished that she had never wrote the comment on the receipt. As well, she claimed that in lieu of the credit card tip, she did leave a cash tip on the table. (Moos, 2013).

****

Black folks' confusion between tipping and tithing has the potential to escalate to unnecessary extremes. The automatic gratuity policy is always stated on the menu. It is a standard policy at almost any restaurant to add automatic gratuity to large parties. It is basic dining knowledge. Many black folks, Christian or not, believe this rule does not apply to them. They cross out automatic gratuity all the time.

What they don't realize, however, is that it does not matter that they've crossed it out. If they are paying by credit/debit card, the automatic gratuity is already processed and charged when they receive the bill. If they cross it out in an attempt to fill in a different amount or in an attempt to leave cash, the new amount they've written in or the cash they've left becomes an additional tip, as the automatic gratuity is already processed in the bill. So, it is pointless to cross it out. If it is the restaurant's policy to add automatic gratuity for a party of a certain size, they do not remove the automatic gratuity policy especially for one person just because he crossed it out. While going through the trouble of trying to reduce the tip, the patron ends up paying more than intended, not less.

Many black folks speak about faith constantly. Many black folks attempt to convert others into religious, faith-based ideologies yet do not practice or put into action the faith they themselves so loudly vocalize. Christianity has an ultimate message of giving, of service to mankind. To use it as an excuse *not* to give and to be disrespectful to others is a blatant contradiction to its teachings.

The Foreign Exchange

A 2015 article from the Washington Post mentions a tipping survey facilitated by TippingResearch.com. Of about 1,000 servers surveyed from different parts of America, 34 percent rated black diners as "very bad" tippers. An additional 36 percent rated black customers as "below average" tippers (Lynn & Brewster, 2015). In essence, 70 percent of those surveyed agreed that black folks suck when it comes to showing financial gratitude at the table. The same statistics also revealed that an overwhelming 98 percent of survey participants rated white diners "average" or "above average," (Lynn & Brewster, 2015).

Does this mean that white diners are better than black diners? Of course not. It means that white diners know about proper etiquette and tipping more than black diners because they have been doing it longer. That's why the entire dining experience feels a little foreign to black people. It *is* foreign. The American restaurant is a European ideal. The cooking schools are European. The recipes are European. The language is European. The entire culture, the entire fine dining experience is a European endeavor. The very concept of tipping itself was also adopted from Europe, dating back to the 17th century (Jayaraman, 2016). White folks have had hundreds of years to solidify the system and benefit from the servitude. Black folks are simply new to the restaurant playing field.

Although black folks are disconnected from the European culture that is fine dining, they share some interesting things in common with European diners themselves. It is as if the dining experience is so foreign to black people, they act like foreigners in their own country when they go out to eat.

Black folks and Europeans share amazingly similar dining characteristics. Serving blacks and serving European foreigners requires the same patience, the same diligence. Neither understands the menu. The foreigner simply can't understand English. Black folks simply refuse to read the menu. Neither can decide what to order. Foreigners have to question many items before ordering. Black folks have to question many items before ordering. Both need extra attention. The foreigner needs more attention because he is, well, foreign. Serving the foreign guest takes more time. It may be difficult to understand the broken English they speak, or they may not understand the particulars of how service works at a certain restaurant. Black folks need the extra attention for recooks, modifications and special requests. Then, ultimately...neither tips well. The difference is, the foreigners are, well, foreign...and do not necessarily understand how the American hospitality industry works. Most likely, when they tip, they mean well, and if the tip is short, it is because of a misunderstanding of how tips work in the USA. Black folks are American citizens who helped build this country yet still suffer from the same lack of understanding.

In Europe, servers are paid more per hour, and the tips left by customers are only supplemental to their wage. Tips are extra money, on top of a decent hourly wage. In America, however, all servers make the $2.13 and greatly depend on the tips from the public as the major part of their income. Dick Rivera, former chairman of the National Restaurant Association, reported in a 2012 article for the *Chicago Tribune* that, "European countries include a service charge on customers' bills and pay servers a straight salary; in the U.S., by contrast, restaurants pay a lower base wage and customers provide a gratuity (or "tip") to waiters and waitresses based on the quality of service received."

In fact, supporters of the increase in minimum wage to $10 an hour cite tipped employees as one of the primary reasons the minimum wage should be increased. Legislators believe that "restaurant employees are squeaking by on nothing more than a 'subminimum' wage plus whatever 'gifts' the customer hands over," (Rivera, 2012). In this regard, America is the polar opposite of Europe. While tipped employees in Europe can expect a decent base wage on which they can survive, their American counterparts do not have the luxury of such an expectation. By contrast, in America, the base hourly wage is merely supplemental to the tipped income. The American base income of $2.13 per hour is often disregarded as chump change or gas money, rather than real income which can be used to pay bills.

Gina Deluca of WiserWaitress.com further explains,

> Unlike Europe, where servers are often paid a set hourly wage, the most common and accepted way to pay servers in the US is through Tips. Some employers are allowed to pay servers a special low sub minimum wage ($2.13) and diners are expected to leave a tip that is based off a percentage of the total amount of the check. The customary rate is 15 to 20 percent. Although diners are free to leave nothing at all and the tip system is voluntary, leaving a tip has become an integral part of US dining culture. Restaurants have an unwritten agreement with the dining public to pay for service by leaving a tip and thus subsidizing the wage of the server. Most restaurants in Europe and other parts of the world do not grant the diner

> this option, they simply integrate a service charge into the price of the meal (Deluca, 2010).

This is why Europeans tip differently. Their tipping system is different. It has evolved into one whereby their restaurant workers are paid an hourly wage. When they tip in Europe, they don't tip very much because tipping is not an obligation of the public. When many Europeans visit American fine dining restaurants, they expect that the American workers are receiving the same decent wage as their European counterparts. Most of them have no idea that the servers are only making $2.13 per hour, working strictly off tips to survive.

Europeans are not the only foreigners who often shortchange their servers. Many Africans, Asians and Hispanics who visit the American restaurant world have trouble with the tipping concept as well. Tipping among foreigners is so disproportionate that there are cases of some American restaurants having added automatic gratuity to foreigners' checks to ensure their servers are tipped properly. Of course, it is an unjust tactic to force foreigners to tip, but some restaurants have felt desperate enough to do so, risking law suits and negative media exposure in the process (Kavoussi, 2012).

Amidst this bizarre and crazy exchange, there is a complete disconnect between the understanding of the patron and the expectation of the server. The lack of understanding surrounding the proper way to tip in American restaurants appears to affect any party not originally connected to the unspoken pact—the one between the black server and white patron. The American tipping narrative has been so deeply penetrated by the black server-white patron relationship that, when any other table dynamic exists, proper tipping becomes a problem. As black citizens step more and more into the role of patron, rather than that of the service worker, it frustrates the historical dynamic in the same way. It is easier for workers to excuse foreigners for their lack of knowledge regarding tipping, but it is much more difficult to accept the same lack of knowledge from black people...because they live in America and should know better.

This level of ignorance creates a sense of urgency among the tipped employees in the food and beverage industry. It is crucial for the public to understand the essence of tipping and why proper tipping is so valuable to the entire social structure of American society. It is important for all citizens to, at least, attempt to understand how the system works, if they choose to participate in it. Participation includes taking an active part in the collective human exchange of currency. It also involves releasing the shared apathy many display towards the well-being of the fellow man. Most importantly, the dining guest must understand how tipping goes beyond the dining experience, affecting everyone, especially the tipper himself. It allows the person who shows love to have love reflected back into his own life.

Removal of Tipping System

It is rather ironic that America adopted its tipping system from one that started in Europe, while countries in Europe have changed their laws and moved forward with paying their restaurant workers an hourly wage. American restaurants, however, still hold fast to their antiquated beginnings. They justify the continuation of the system with whatever facts support their cause.

For instance, the tipping system helps keep restaurant menu prices down. While the menu prices cover the cost of the food, they also cover other restaurant expenses such as rent, utilities, food delivery and other bills (Holt, 2013). If the restaurant were responsible for tipping its staff, too, it would have to offset this wage by inflating the prices of the food and beverages on the menu.

Evidence of this menu inflation exists in those ambitious restaurants in California and New York, attempting to put an end to customer tipping altogether. "In Los Angeles, the Bel-Air Bar + Grill announced it will increase menu prices, eliminate tipping and increase employee wages" to ensure all their staff maintained a fair wage (Harris, 2016). As well, popular chef Danny Meyer eliminated tipping policies in his New York restaurants, favoring instead, higher hourly wages for his employees, which in turn meant higher prices for items on his menu.

There is much debate in the restaurant industry regarding whether the elimination of tipping will be beneficial to restaurants, their staff and their customers. In some cases, the non-tipping experiment has led to loss of customers, as well as loss of employees (Zagorsky, 2016). Customers do not understand the reasoning behind the inflated prices. All they know is that the prices went up. Ultimately, they hesitate to return to a restaurant where prices have suddenly increased with no explanation. Servers want money. Period. Apparently, they would rather gamble on flashing an award-winning smile and bet on the good graces of the public to pay their incomes instead of receiving predictable, steady pay, directly from the boss. And evidently, they make more money this way.

In Washington, D.C., new legislation was passed by 55 percent of voters in June 2018, eliminating the current trend of $3.33 per hour minimum for tipped employees. The new law was to help the workers secure the same standard minimum wage of $12.50 shared by all the workers in the nation's capital city. The Restaurant Opportunities Center (ROC) United sponsored this campaign in efforts "to help restaurant workers recover stolen tips and wages, and win protection from sexual harassment," (Nirappil & Carman, 2018). The ROCU believes the only way to decrease sexual harassment is to increase minimum wage from $2.13 an hour to a decent hourly wage, so that female servers (who are the majority of the claimants) don't have to rely on the favors of men by looking sexy and enduring sexist circumstances just to get money from customers and make a decent living (ROCUnited.org).

However, the National Restaurant Association and the Restaurant Association of Metropolitan Washington both opposed the initiative. Many business owners and thousands of restaurant workers themselves, whom Initiative 77 was supposed to help, fought to have the legislation repealed (Nirappil & Carman, 2018). Just four months later, in October the same year, the D.C. city council overturned the initiative. Neither the restaurant owners nor the tipped employees wanted to make the change. Owners feared the higher prices would run off the customers, while workers "feared their bosses would cut hours or customers would be stingy with tips if the measure became law," (Nirappil & Carman, 2018).

This is not surprising in a society predicated on money, class and one-upmanship. Many argue that, even as the policies change from state to state and servers begin to receive higher hourly wages, some customers will still embrace the classist need to throw in a little extra to *the help*. "California, Oregon, Washington, Alaska, Nevada, Montana and Minnesota have had laws for decades requiring businesses to pay all workers the same minimum wage regardless of tips. Restaurateurs in those states, as well as researchers, say diners continue to tip despite higher menu prices designed to cover the increased labor costs," (Nirappil & Carman, 2018).

The history of tipping in America is deeply rooted in ideals far more complex than the new notion of fair wages for all. Americans need the tipping system to continue the economic divide, to distinguish one bank account from another, to separate one group from another and maintain the financial hierarchy that they've come to know, love and depend upon. Servers depend on the twisted nature of this economic psychology to offset the minimum wage by collecting heavy tips from customers who carry the guilt of having too much money. Obviously, the varied tips collected from the American public's moral battle with greed and guilt outweigh the minimum wage pay the boss is offering.

Of course, fair wages for all should be the bottom line for all employers. It is noble that restaurant owners and chefs alike are taking a stand to ensure their employees earn a decent wage, especially when their staffs are taken advantage of in so many different ways, in so many different arenas. It is clear that the solution here is for the restaurants to spend more money on staff pay without increasing menu prices, which would mean less dividends for the restaurant. However, decreasing their own revenue for the sake of staff and customers has never been an option in this fight. Some, like Jamie Leeds from JL Restaurant Group in Virginia, claim they've run the numbers and eliminating the tipped wage would force them to change their entire business model (Nirappil & Carman, 2018). The tipping system is so delicately interwoven into this industry that both the workers and the restaurants insist they cannot survive without it.

Nonetheless, the fight against tipping continues. The Trump Administration has proposed that the Department of Labor pass yet another law to regulate the tipping standard. Those who support this law claim it will help evenly distribute wages among tipped staff and kitchen workers. However, under this new policy, management would be able to keep all tips from tipped workers and redistribute them however they saw fit. Even worse, the law was written with such vague language that supervisors and managers would be able to even keep tips for themselves (Scheiber, 2018).

Those who oppose it point out that an estimated $6 billion dollars would be taken from tipped workers and put into the hands of companies, who simply want more control over their workers' tips so they themselves won't have to pay them (Horsley, 2018). After public backlash over the new proposal, the Department of Labor revamped its initial plan—this time, ensuring employers could not pocket any tips themselves (Horsley, 2019).

Restaurant companies insist on repeating history over and over. First, it was the tipping system itself, then the tip-out tip sharing method. Now, it is a new proposal for tip pooling. Each is merely a progression of the previous idea, and each is a new way for employers to avoid spending their own money. They pay themselves, then keep creating new ways to force everyone else to pay everyone else. The removal of the tipping system is a redundant attempt at revolution by those who control the industry, constantly claiming their efforts are to help the people. Yet, the revolution is continuously interrupted by the same people who supposedly benefit from its success.

Could Americans be so caught up into traditions of status and class in society, that the tipping system is here to stay? The future holds the answers, and only time will tell.

Why Twenty?

The definition of the standard tip has changed. Whereas before in previous decades, a diner could drop a couple of bucks on a two-egg plate and call it day, the entire restaurant industry is different now. Everything has evolved. The very concept of the restaurant itself has changed. The amount of services offered has increased. The menu prices have inflated. The amount of work the server is required to do is greater than before. The entire restaurant experience has changed. The only thing that has not changed with the times is the server's hourly wage and the dependency on tips to pay the bills. This is why the 20 percent tip has become such a big deal.

In today's American dining times, an 18 to 20 percent tip has become the basic standard for all dining service. For excellent and superior service, many patrons tip even higher. Twenty percent helps to level the *paying field*, so that servers are working for actual money, rather than working for crumbs or working for free. Any tip less than 20 percent is like a stiff middle finger to the server and all the other tip-supported staff, without whom the beautiful dining experience would not have been possible.

For the sake of clarity, the 20 percent tip pays for work that patrons may not necessarily get to witness take place before their very eyes. Contrary to what customers might see or believe, most of the work of the waitstaff is performed, not at the dining table but behind the scenes. The repetitive fetching of water and condiments and the constant refilling of beverages can seem simple tasks, but they are often performed out of view of the customer. Diners have no clue how complicated some of these tasks can become, especially while working a busy shift with dozens of other staff who all need the same thing at the same time. Refilling a cola is only a simple task when the restaurant has not run out of cola, when the fountain machine is working properly, when the ice machine is not on the fritz, when there are clean glasses available. Insert any of these inevitable variables into a busy night at any restaurant, and suddenly, refilling a cola can become an impossible task which can ruin the flow of an entire evening.

Ensuring the order was entered properly into the computer system, the communication with the staff and the kitchen to further ensure the correctness of the order—restaurant guests do not get to see these things happening. The checking for timely delivery of food, the checking to make sure each meal is exactly the way the guest requested, the demand to have it corrected if necessary...who at the table is a witness to all this? The server is responsible for making sure the entire visit flows smoothly, that each course is delivered fluidly behind the other. The server performs all these tasks, and so much more, but out of sight. Most guests are clueless as to how much effort is required to serve them.

Perhaps in this case, out of sight is indeed out of mind. Because patrons do not see all the work performed by the server, they pay no thought to it. They do not understand everything entailed because they don't see it all go down. They see servers drop off plates, pick up plates. It appears the drop off/pick up is all there is to the job. Why should people tip 20 percent for that?

And bottles of wine, why should people tip 20 percent for that? All the server did was bring the wine to the table and open it up, right? Wrong. The server may have had to move mountains just for your wine service. It is not okay to buy expensive wine and skip tipping on the wine service. Some customers believe they should not have to tip on wine, opting to only tip on the food instead. However, wine service is extremely cumbersome and often requires more work than serving the food. It entails several or all of the following:

Seeking out the correct bottle of wine.

In some establishments, a server simply rings up the bottle of wine in the computer system, then retrieves it from the bar from the knowledgeable bartender who knows where the wine is located. In many other cases, however, the server is responsible for the scavenger hunt that ensues from trying to locate a single bottle of wine. Depending on the restaurant's storage system, the bottle could be any damn where—the attic, the basement or anywhere in between. It may take a server more than 10 minutes just to find the correct bottle or even longer to discover that bottle is out of stock.

Seeking out the appropriate wine glasses for the varietal served.

The hunt for clean, polished wine glasses can take longer and be more exhausting than the search for the bottle of wine itself. Restaurants only carry a certain amount of glasses, period. On a busy night, they may all be in use at once. Servers spend a great deal of time merely waiting on clean glasses to come out the dishwasher, which then must be dried and polished before delivered to the table.

Ensuring the wine glasses are clean and polished, and polishing them if necessary.

Even in the event that clean wine glasses are available and clearly stocked up for use, the glasses may still be blemished with water streaks and caked-on food from the dishwasher. Each server is responsible for checking wine glasses for cleanliness and ensuring each is polished before dropping it before a guest.

Carrying multiple glasses at once to the table and placing them in a certain position for each drinking guest.

Requires finesse.

Opening the wine professionally...while simultaneously engaging in bullshit small talk.

Requires using both left and right brain simultaneously.

Pouring a taste for the host and awaiting approval.

Requires patience. Sometimes lots.

Decanting the wine.

Aged wine develops sediments of grape solids which gather at the bottom of the bottle until opened for enjoyment. Therefore, older bottles of wine highly benefit from a decanting process. During this process, the aged wine is transferred from its original bottle to a large, rounded, glass vessel made particularly for trapping the sediment and preventing it from entering the wine glass when poured. A server's duty is to retrieve the required items and perform these steps for the guest at the table.

Pouring the wine in exact measurements for each guest, without wasting a single drop on the table.

Requires the ability to eyeball a 3-ounce pour into each glass...and the grace of a ballerina.

Refilling the glasses with wine throughout the dinner.

Requires balancing act. Servers must stay in tune with who drank how much wine and gauge who should
get more, while trying to be fair in pouring the wine for all guests.

Clearing the empty bottle and corresponding glasses from the table.

More tip-deserving work.

If the party orders another bottle, this process must be repeated from top to bottom. So, the thought that one might skip tipping for this is nonsense. Again, customers do not see all the work that goes into serving them. So much work is completed behind the scene. If patrons want expensive wine, they should be prepared to tip for it—just like food. Customers often have unwarranted ideals regarding tipping which they use to take liberty *not* to do the right thing, *not* to give what they should—excuses *not* to pay. This is the ultimate problem with the whole tipping system. When the public is responsible for the income of the worker, they can adopt whatever rationale or create any excuse they choose to *not* tip a server and thereby withhold the income. Meanwhile, the workers are pleading with the public to step up the tip game to match the current times.

Serving is not rocket science, but it's not recess on the playground either. It takes a great deal of focus, clarity, communication, brains and muscle. A flawless dinner—where everything that was ordered was delivered to the table correctly, where the bill listed exactly what was ordered—was not happenstance or coincidental. A server made that happen.

Why 20 percent? Three words: inflation and expectation. David Holt, a server for over a dozen years, so eloquently explains in a *Denver Post* article,

> The cost of living has increased nearly tenfold since 1950. The cost of a meal at a casual-dining restaurant, however, has only increased by sevenfold in that time. That means that for a server to have the same standard of living, the tip percentage has to have increased about 40 percent from what it was in 1950. Since the standard tip in 1950 was 10 percent, that means that it needs to have increased by about 4 percent to provide the same standard of living.
>
> If this were the only factor, then a standard tip of 15 percent would be just dandy. However, this is not the only factor that has increased the standard tip percentage.
>
> In addition to the change in the relationship between the cost of living and the cost of a meal, the expectations customers have for their servers have changed. People tend to forget that restaurants are selling two products: food *and* service. In 1950, it was not uncommon for a server to have a section of eight or ten tables. Service was prompt and efficient...everyone was happy. This means that in 1950, each table was paying for 10

> percent of a server's time. In 2010, however, customers expect much more. Servers are now expected to refill drinks before they are half-empty, clear dishes as soon as they are used, serve multiple courses, check back frequently, and provide pleasant small talk...servers have less time for other tables. As a result, restaurants have scaled back the size of a server's section to three or four tables. That means that customers today are purchasing 20 percent of a server's time. Since each server only has so much time in an hour, and the demand for that time has increased, the price paid must increase, too—in this case, in the form of an increased tip. If a 10 percent tip purchased 10 percent of a server's time in 1950, then in order to purchase 20 percent, the tip must increase to 20 percent as well (Holt, 2013).

Understand that the more food and drink ordered and the more money spent, the more time and energy it takes for the server to satisfy those requests. There is much more work required to ring in the order and ensure it comes out correctly, as ordered. There is more running back and forth for refills and condiments. Until a payment system is devised which pays a server strictly based on how much time he or she spends with each table, it makes natural sense that the tip should correspond to the amount of the total bill, as the bill ultimately constitutes how much time it took to serve the party. The 20 percent figure did not mysteriously fall out of the sky, it is structured from calculations of inflation over time in conjunction with an ever-evolving dining culture. Hopefully, a more understanding dining public—one more knowledgeable about tipping culture, will care enough about those who serve them to make the adjustment to tipping 20 percent. Fear, perhaps, is all that is left to conquer.

Overcoming Fear

Most Americans revolve their entire lives around money. It is the foremost preoccupation of the American people—the dreaming of it, the acquisition of it...having it, saving it, spending it. For many black people, however, life revolves around *the lack* of money. Not having enough money is the central theme around which most black people struggle to survive. The idea that one does not have or will not have enough money for survival is a lingering thought, a permanent idea in the daily lives of the American poor. Many black folks, even while dressed immaculately and perhaps driving a nice car, are struggling well below the poverty line to make ends meet and put food on the table. Statistics show that African-Americans endure the highest poverty rate among all ethnic groups in America, with over 45 percent of young black children living in poverty (Economic Poverty Institute, StateofWorkingAmerica.org, n.d.).

The understanding of money is passed down to each culture over generations of time. Black people and their relationship with money is no exception. There are misconceptions and fears regarding money that have been deeply embedded into the African-American psyche over hundreds of years. Until these fears are understood and conquered, black folks will remain disconnected from healthy relationships with currency. As most black people do not even realize that there is a problem at all with the way they view and handle money, these damaging ideas about money may take many an entire lifetime to unravel. Until these detrimental ideas are corrected, they will forever prevent black people from living in abundant joy.

This current outlook towards money is controlling the lives of black people from multiple angles. How much money one has, or doesn't have, determines everything—what one has, where one goes, what one chooses to do in life. It controls everything. Homes are foreclosed, automobiles are repossessed and bills fall behind because people believe there is not enough money to pay them. Lifelong friendships and great relationships are destroyed over distorted beliefs and expectations about money. People who have loved each other for decades will allow some tidbit over money to completely destroy all they have built and accomplished together. Again, it seems money controls it all.

Hidden within these misconceptions is the belief that money is finite. Money is believed to be a physical, tangible object that is counted, lost, found, earned and spent—designed and printed by the government and systematically distributed to black people in much smaller amounts. In this regard, it represents something which is limited, scarce. It must be physically embraced and carefully held on to. So, of course, if people believe there is only so much money to go around, then they become afraid to let go of it. They become afraid to spend, afraid to give.

Though difficult for many to conceptualize, the truth is...money is not merely dollars and cents. It is not simply metal coins and colored paper. Money is an energy. It is a true currency that circulates throughout a society. It can control the people or be controlled by the people—all depending on its understanding by the people. Money is like a flowing river, supplying flora and fauna to a local village, then stretching out into the sea...only to return back to the village teeming with more life. The river is simply a vessel, but it is important because it carries joy and happiness to the people. The physical money one can hold in his hands is not as important as the spiritual livelihood the money can provide. And so, the money is simply a vessel, important because of what it carries to the people—sustenance, joy, comfort, happiness and fulfillment. What people really want is freedom—freedom to have and do and go and see and experience. In this capitalistic physical reality, money controls the access to all these things. Freedom costs money. Without it, how much can a person have or do or go or see or experience? Very little and next to nothing. It forces a person with little money to scrounge for simple freedoms that others seem to be enjoying without any difficulty at all. Dining at nice restaurants is one of those simple freedoms. Black people want to enjoy the dining experience just like everyone else. However, many black folks do not have the money to afford these price-inflated places. As a result, they must make financial sacrifices to patronize them.

With regard to tipping, why would a person who believes money is scarce add extra money to an already overpriced bill, when they are not obligated to do so?

The fact that black folks don't tip is not a black people problem. This is an American problem. It is a direct result of racism, discrimination and inequality. Here is a country which prides itself as being the greatest nation in the world while forcibly disallowing a specific group of people to advance in culture, in education, in economics. America has told black people that they are free, yet it has dispositioned them to experience no freedom, while forcing them to watch everyone else have and do and go and see and experience whatever they choose. Therefore, when black folks do dare to experience the simple freedom of dining out, they do so with cultural, educational and economic disadvantages. They show up uninformed and uneducated, attempting to have a meal while wading a sea of racism, discrimination and inequality. The entire endeavor becomes an exercise in fear. They don't follow the rules, and they don't tip. They end up bearing the weight of *the bad guy*—the worst patrons ever. All they were trying to do is enjoy a simple freedom.

Of course, there are obvious flaws in the entire American system. However, instead of waiting on the American system to change, black folks must change their personal belief system. Black people can begin to overcome fears about money with a simple adjustment in what they believe.

Brokeness, lack and suffering are all manmade ideas and have no place in the reality of mankind unless man believes them to be real. If there is belief that there is no money, then that belief will manifest itself in man's reality. The penny-pinching habits of hoarding money and saving money only assist in perpetuating fear, and they keep the continuous flow of money at bay and forever out of arm's reach. The age-old adage of "use it or lose it" applies to money just like everything else.

Tipping is a perfect way to exercise the power of abundance and constant supply. When one gives, and gives freely and happily, he is practicing his faith in the belief that money is not only plentiful but accessible by him in great supply for whatever he desires. As difficult as it may be for many to accept this fact, it is a fundamental truth in this thing called life. It is universal law. It is the greatest way to enjoy the simple freedoms—to have and go and do and see and experience—without having to beg and plead and march and lobby and struggle and fight for the pursuit of liberty.

Even more important than overcoming the fear of money is adopting the practice of love. Love is the opposite of fear, and love is the answer in all things.

Everyone is connected. There is no coincidence. Each meeting with another human is an opportunity to learn something or share something or realize something. Each person stands to evolve from the interaction. When people choose to dine out, they must understand that the timeliness of circumstances in someone else's life will always line up with the timeliness of circumstances of their own.

Through this universal dance, people will attract both their table and their server. Whoever that person is, he or she will have something to learn or something to share, that will forward each person on his or her personal life journey. In order for this to happen, people must be open to receive the benefit from the exchange. This cannot be accomplished if people do not respect the attracted connection or the potential relationship for the new people they meet. Black folks are many times so preoccupied with money and their own survival that they become completely insensitive to the existence of other people. They become inconsiderate of the lives of others and numb to the needs of anyone other than themselves.

Spiritual livelihood cannot be obtained with physical money only. Spiritual livelihood is also fostered by timely connections and healthy relationships. While people are only focused on the money and what the money will bring, they neglect crucial relationships and ignore important connections, and they miss out on the divine messages others may have to share with them. The connections made and the relationships built with other humans on the planet are crucial to personal liberty and human pursuits of happiness.

When people learn to value other people, they do not gravitate toward the disrespect and dismissal of them. They become more considerate of others. When customers start to care more about people than money, the appropriate tipping will naturally follow.

Many patrons have been looking at the entire idea of tipping backwards. People think tipping is about giving up something and handing it over to someone else, that tipping is about paying the server. However, tipping is not about the other person as much as it is about the tipper himself.

Tipping is akin to forgiveness. Forgiveness is not about doing something for someone else. Forgiveness is not a favor granted somebody, nor is it some mercy bestowed upon another. Forgiveness is a self-pardon. People forgive for the sake of themselves, so that they can be free to welcome peace and happiness into their lives and move forward. Tipping and forgiveness are similar in this way. On the surface, tipping appears to be about the receiver, but it is more about the giver and his beliefs about money and his relationship with the world.

When one offers a tip to another, although the money benefits the other person, the giver receives the ultimate reward. Giving freely opens people up to receive just so. Spending money freely is a testament to the fact that it is available to spend. There is comfort in letting it go because of the belief that there is more available. Through a greater comfort with money, people are more apt to respect and value the connections and relationships they create with other people. People are crucial to the alignment of the human experience. People are more valuable than money.

Understandably, for many black folks, fine dining restaurants are newly chartered territory. Nevertheless, because so many African-American ancestors fought and died for the right to explore this new land and settle therein, it is important to handle the experience with respect and pride.

Otherwise, why die fighting to sit in the damn restaurant in the first place?

6

BLACK FOLKS DON'T UNDERSTAND

Exploring Etiquette

The Do's and Don'ts of Dining

Manners are a sensitive awareness of the feelings of others.
If you have that awareness, you have good manners, no matter what fork you use.
—Emily Post

ARRIVAL

DO some research on the place first.

Find out the operation hours. Scan the menu so that you have an idea of what you like. Know the parking situation before you arrive. Have cash on hand to pay the valet if necessary.

DO be on time for your reservation.

After you are 30 minutes late for a reservation, please do not expect the red carpet treatment once you arrive. It is very possible that you lost your table to someone else. Time is money, and a restaurant can only wait so long on guests that may or may not be coming. One late party can jeopardize the flow of the restaurant for the entire evening. If you are late and the restaurant is nice enough to still accommodate your party, be grateful. Show some gratitude. And if you are going to be late, please call the restaurant and let them know so that arrangements can be made for your late arrival. Otherwise, you and your party may find yourselves assed out.

DO show up for your reservation with your complete party.

Text them. Call them. Video chat. Sit in the car and rearrange your cell phone pictures until they get there. Do whatever it takes to coordinate your arrival with that of your guests, so that you are all there together. Many restaurants do not seat you unless the entire party has arrived. When the bar is full, there is no place else to go, so you and your party may be just hanging around outside, or hanging around inside, and in the way no less. Be prepared to wait in the car or wait at the bar. To avoid such an awkward disposition, refer to the previous rule. Be on time—together.

DO abide by the rules of the house.

Don't try to change the restaurant's policies. If they do not seat parties larger than eight people, don't try to negotiate the rules to accommodate you and your party. If they do not honor substitutions, simply don't request them. If they close at 10 p.m., don't show up at 9:45. Everybody is shutting down and ready to go home, then here you come. They will only take your order because they have to. You will receive mediocre food and even worse service.

TABLE ETIQUETTE

DON'T rearrange the furniture, chairs and tables to accommodate your party.

It is important to make your reservation as accurately as possible. If you request seating for 20, you should show up with 20. Please do not invite 30 people and expect the restaurant to work some sort of seating miracle for 10 extra unexpected guests. In cases where it is feasible, the restaurant staff may be able to add an additional seat or table. Rather than moving the furniture yourself, please see a server, host or manager for assistance with your seating needs.

If you start a brand new friendship with a neighboring table, and you would like to merge parties, please talk to a staff member about your new seating requirements. Please do not push tables together or move chairs around. These work tasks are jobs of the restaurant staff. It is important to allow the staff to accommodate your needs. Why? Some tables are not meant to match others. Putting them together could create unknown danger to the guest. Some chairs are table-specific and arranged accordingly. The seat height of one chair may be intended for the height of only one particular table. Moving this chair to a different table might make dining extremely uncomfortable for the guest. Without knowing, the pushing of two tables together and the moving of chairs could impede a busy passage or create a fire hazard. It is best to allow the restaurant staff to handle the movement of all restaurant furniture.

DON'T squeeze a 5th person into a 4-person booth.

The restaurant has been setup in such a way as to provide comfort and ease of access to the guest, as well as efficient delivery of food and beverage to the guest. Tables are setup to accommodate a certain number of people. Squeezing too many people into a booth disallows room for the plateware and glassware to properly fit on the table and creates a great deal of stress on the server.

DON'T request an invisible menu.

Ladies and gentleman, the menu in front of you is the menu that is available at that time. If you saw something online, and it is not available at the restaurant when you visit, lighten up. It happens. Chefs change the menu seasonally, sometimes randomly even. The websites hardly ever keep up with what's going on inside the actual place. Use the website as a general guide, but understand the prices and the menu may slightly vary from what you find at the restaurant itself. If you show up for dinner on Valentine's Day, don't be upset if you suddenly discover a specially created menu for that special day. And don't be surprised if the "regular" menu is unavailable. Simply, choose a different item from the available menu, or politely leave and go somewhere else.

Whatever you do, don't fight with the staff because you can't have what you want. The servers have no control over the menu whatsoever, and asking a chef any ridiculous questions about it will surely piss him or her off. Pissing off the chef is not a goal of any person working in the restaurant—not even the managers want to piss off the chef. Making a big stank about the menu will not change the situation. And don't try to use the opportunity to get something for free. If the restaurant offers you something complimentary, please feel free to accept. However, don't expect a discount or a freebie because the menu is changed, different or unavailable.

DON'T use your cell phone at the dinner table.

Fine dining restaurants train their servers to be respectful of guests who are on the telephone. Therefore, if you are on the telephone when you first sit down at a table, then it may take a few minutes longer before you are approached by anyone. Please do not take offense. It is rude to interrupt a guest while he/she is on the phone and more appropriate and polite to simply wait until the call has ended before approaching the table. Otherwise, the server would be standing aimlessly over the table, waiting for you to finish your phone conversation, and perhaps eavesdropping meanwhile.

It is best to simply refrain from using your cell phone at the dining table anyway. You are not using good table manners when you are on the phone during a meal. And for heaven's sake, please refrain from watching videos and playing video games. Being on the phone takes the guest out of the present moment and away from the current experience. It is rude to those in your party, as well as inconsiderate of those seated nearby. If you must take a call while dining, kindly excuse yourself from the table. Find a great place outside to chat quickly or even go into the rest room or bar area to have a conversation on the phone.

DON'T request hot water to soak your silverware in at the table.
Asking your server to bring you hot water to soak your silverware symbolizes a lack of trust of the restaurant. It's inappropriate and just downright tacky. If you don't trust that the silverware is clean, why trust anything in the restaurant at all?

If you have overeaten, DON'T lay your head down on the table nor lay down in the booth.
It takes a certain kind of carelessness to allow one's body to lazy itself enough to actually lay down in a restaurant booth while others in the party are finishing up their meals. The same is true of laying one's head down at a public dinner table. One should never find himself falling asleep during dinner at a restaurant—no matter how stuffed one may be. And one should never intoxicate himself to the point of sloppy drunkenness whereby he has fallen asleep at the table.

If you have overeaten and a puffy cloud of sleepiness has hovered over your physical body, it is a good time to take a walk to the bathroom or even a walk outside. Dust off the fatigue however it suits you best and return to the table with the intention of leaving soon. Or, just politely excuse yourself from the party, and call it a night. Your party, as well as the restaurant staff, will prefer this to you laying down on the table or in the booth.

COMMUNICATION WITH SERVER

DON'T be rude.

As already detailed, there are many things about the fine dining experience that black folks simply do not know. There are other things, however, that are simply common sense—that we should know but somehow do not seem to exercise when we actually get to the table. Common sense, along with its moral compass, gets smothered under our need to be oppressive and feel superior to others.

The exchange between the guest and the server should always be pleasant. There is never a need for inappropriate words or ill-mannered conduct from a guest. It is important to be respectful of your server. A little bit a patience and a lot of respect will go a very long way in guaranteeing a great restaurant experience.

In her book entitled *Emily Post's Etiquette—Manners for a New World*, Ms. Post states the following under the heading, "Waiters are People, Too,"

> Much of the success and enjoyment of your meal hinges on your interaction with your waiter or waitress...a polite diner will treat them with respect...Treating a server as a robot or servant is unforgivably rude, and an imperious or condescending manner shows you not as superior but as a jerk, (2011).

Ms. Post hits the nail right on the head. The server is the primary point of contact for the diner. The server is the point of reference for all guests in the restaurant. Because he or she holds such a pivotal position in the restaurant, the server is the most valuable player—someone guests should want on their team. If some life situation has upset or angered you before or during your visit, check yourself before transferring that vibration to the server and to others around you.

DON'T be impatient.

Your server is trained to check on you and your party within a matter of minutes. Many restaurants require the guest, once seated, to be greeted with a beverage within 60 seconds. It is important that you, as a guest, allow the server to come to you. When you have a question or a need, simply wait on the server to return. Please don't yell or holler at your server from way across the room. Do not track your server down. And most certainly, unless you are going to go potty, please do not get up out of your seat. Simply wait on the server to return to request what you need, or ask a staff member walking by to send your server over to your table. If you find your server incompetent or incapable, request a manager and politely share your grievance.

DON'T run your server to death.

One of the best ways to sabotage your own dining experience is to run your server all over the restaurant. It is not okay to ask your server for something every single time she approaches your table. Doing so will almost always result in poor service—poor service for which the server will be blamed when it is actually the diner at fault.

If you need something new, something else, every time your server comes to your table, then this means you have not given the proper attention required to place your order and you have not given enough thought to your needs. For example, perhaps you order a glass of sweet tea. When your waiter returns with the sweet tea, you then request a straw. When the waiter returns with the straw, you ask for extra lemons. When the lemons arrive, you need extra ice. Then when the waiter returns with the glass of ice, you realize you need more sweetener. This is a disastrous way to request service. At some point, your requests will cease to arrive in a timely manner.

Remember, there are other tables your server must support while simultaneously providing great service to you. By requesting something new, something else, each time your server comes around, you also negatively affect the service those other tables receive, which may potentially decrease the tips that server receives. On top of all this, running your server this way makes him feel like your personal slave. No one can deliver great service while feeling this way.

Try to assess your needs before you order. Then when the friendly server arrives, you can request everything at once. It is very important that you respectfully communicate with your server throughout the entire dining experience, rather than treat her as a gofer. This will help to ensure a lovely dining excursion, not only for yourself, but for others around you as well. The restaurant has choreographed the entire dining experience for you. All you have to do is simply enjoy the dance.

Take the opportunity, whenever warranted, to request a manager to report how GREAT the service was, instead of how bad. Let the manager know, with details and particulars, why you enjoyed the service so much. Spread love.

TWO PEOPLE, TWO CHAIRS

I didn't know she was Madame Co-Host at first. Madame Co-Host and her friend sat at a table in my section on a balcony in Buckhead Atlanta. It was a beautiful day—early evening, and the sun seemed skeptical about its daily demise over the city. Madame Co-Host and her friend were a party of two, sitting at a table for two people.

After approaching the table to greet the two ladies, Madame Co-Host asked for an extra chair. Immediately, I inquired whether or not another person would be joining the two of them. Madame Co-Host responded sharply, "No." She was rather short and dismissive with her reply. It seemed as if she did not want to entertain any questions from me, she only wanted me to step and fetch the chair.

As a bona fide server, employed at that establishment, I knew that to add another chair to her table would create a fire hazard. The balcony was already set up for the maximum occupancy, and there were no extra balcony chairs available. Meaning, every balcony chair was already accounted for and already placed where it was supposed to be. There were no extra balcony chairs stashed in some back closet somewhere.

The nature of the dilemma combined with the dismissive attitude of Madame Co-Host initiated a temporary memory loss in my brain and caused me to intentionally forget about her chair request. I left to place drink orders for the ladies. When I returned with the drinks, I carried on with the evening and took their orders as usual. I mentioned nothing of the chair she had requested. I had intentionally forgot about it, remember. As far as I was concerned, I had attempted to accommodate her request, but I needed more information to carry out the order. When she snapped at me, I stereotyped her as The Black Woman in Chapter 4. Because of this, I lost all concern for her request for the extra chair. So, when I returned with the beverages with no chair and no mention of a chair, Madame Co-Host mentioned it again.

Uppity, she uttered, "I'm still waiting on the chair."

I offered a professional response. "Yes ma'am. To put an extra chair here would impede the passageway and create a fire hazard. If you have another person joining your party, we can try to move you to a larger table."

After peering around the balcony at the empty chairs at other empty tables, Madame Co-Host replied, "What's wrong with just grabbing a chair from another table?"

"Yes ma'am. Those chairs are reserved for incoming reservations. If I remove them from their positions, the guests with reservations would have no seats." Then I lied, "I have management searching to see if there is an extra chair in storage for you." I already knew there were no extra chairs.

Madame Co-Host said nothing.

"Let me go check on that now," I said as an excuse to hurry from the table. I still had no earthly clue what she needed the chair for. She didn't seem to care about the fire hazard.

When I walked back through the balcony again to check on another table, Madame Co-Host stopped me along the way and snapped, "I really need that chair."

I approached another server who was working on the balcony that night as well. I explained the situation with Madame Co-Host and begged for one of the chairs at her table. She was not happy. She did not want to give up one of her chairs. Taking a chair from her meant reducing her table size from a party of four to a party of three, which would jeopardize her incoming reservations. Less table seats means less guests at the table, which means less money spent, which equals a smaller tip. I hated to ask this of her. With great hesitance, she gave up a chair. I took the chair to Madame Co-Host and placed it in the fire hazard passageway.

Out of nowhere came this huge bright canary-colored bag. It was a very, very, very nice bag and obviously very, very, very expensive. Apparently, she had been holding the purse under a jacket in her lap, refusing to let it touch the ground. She gently placed the expensive bag in the fire hazard chair. No acknowledgement to me. No thanks.

I replied in awe, "Wow..." I was mesmerized by the beautiful bag, while simultaneously holding contempt for her for not simply saying in the beginning, "I need a place to sit my bag."

It was more important for her to subordinate me than it was to offer a simple explanation. Madame Co-Host dismissed me as one who was asking too many questions. She offered a just-do-what-I-say attitude towards the situation which made her request difficult to fulfill. Had she answered my question and further communicated her needs, the purse situation could have been quickly and easily resolved and the exchange could have been lovely. I would have immediately understood why the chair was necessary and figured out a proper alternative for her that was suitable for both her purse and the fire hazard. Instead, the confusion over the bag created uneasiness and tension throughout the entire visit. And to top it all off, I had to break bread with the server who helped me. Understanding the sacrifice she made, I gave her 20 bucks to thank her for borrowing a chair from one of her tables.

If Madame Co-Host must have a chair for her expensive handbag, she should request the correct number of seats to accommodate said expensive handbag when requesting a table. This way, the server does not have to impede a passageway nor risk a fire hazard to satisfy her request. As well, no other server unrelated to her experience has to suffer or potentially lose income to accommodate her table needs, nor would I have had to take money from my own tips to pay for it.

PARTY OF 2 + 1 HANDBAG, TOO EXPENSIVE TO TOUCH THE GROUND = PARTY OF 3

TABLE TIME

DON'T camp out.

Understanding appropriate table time is a valuable lesson for people of all races. However, again, it is black folks who exploit this particular opportunity the most. Black folks tend to overstay longer and more often than other people. It is as if they have nowhere else to go.

The average dine out for dinner takes approximately one to two hours. Two hours is a nice lengthy dinner at any restaurant, whether it be upscale or hole-in-the-wall. Often times, a party of black folks will still be occupying a table well over an hour after they have paid the bill. Black people seem to be oblivious to the dinner time table. And those who are aware of this imposition, simply do not care about it at all.

No one ever wants to rush a party out of a restaurant. It is much more desirable that you come in and take your time and have a wonderful experience. However, some folks do not seem to care about overstaying their welcome, and it happens all the time. When customers overstay their welcome, servers huddle in the back of the restaurant as a team, trying to figure out how to make them get up from the table without actually asking them to leave. As long as you are still sitting at a table, until you get up and leave, your server is supposed to check in with you to see if you need anything.

So...you've paid the bill. An hour has passed. You're still sitting there. The server keeps stopping by your table, asking if you need anything. You don't need anything. The server is getting on your last nerve with the constant check-ins. You start to feel some type of way. The server is uncomfortable doing his job. It's awkward.

The server can keep doing her job and keep checking by the table, annoying the hell out of you, until you eventually feel irritated enough to get up and leave. Or, the server can leave you sitting there without checking on you anymore at all, in which case, if you did actually decide to order some dessert or coffee or another cocktail, your server would be nowhere to be found. Again, this is why constant communication with the server is so crucial. Let your server know if you plan to hang out a while and what you may or may not need so that the server can best accommodate the situation without the awkwardness and confusion.

Once everyone in your party has finished eating, what else is there left to do? Once dessert has been finished and cleared from the table, it is time to go. Of course, if you are having after-dinner wine, cocktails or cordials, this is different because you are still ordering. However, if you know for certain that you plan on ordering nothing else, keep it moving. Take the precious time you deserve to digest your food, have a few more laughs and bring your dinner to a close. Then pay your bill, tip properly, and leave the restaurant. Time is money.

In addition, if you notice the restaurant is extremely busy, and perhaps there are dozens of people waiting to be seated, this is not the time to linger at the table, twiddling thumbs, doing nothing. Get up and go. This is actually a wonderful opportunity to be considerate of others and allow someone else to dine. Nevertheless, if you find yourself still at the table an hour or so after payment, leave an extra tip. Anything less is disrespectful and inconsiderate.

THE TWELVE-HOUR SWEET TEA

The restaurant opens at 11:00am and closes at 10:00pm. A table of four black women arrive at the restaurant at 11:15am. The four women are seated at Table 2. This is the very first table of the day for Table 2 server, who happens to be working a double-shift this particular day. A double shift means that Table 2 server will be working from open to close. After the restaurant closes at 10:00pm, Table 2 server may not leave the restaurant until after midnight when all his/her closing duties are completed.

Each of the four women orders a beverage, and they all share an appetizer. They talk and giggle and talk some more. A couple of hours pass. Meanwhile, they request repeated free refills on the beverages they ordered. More free bread. More chips. More free drinks. After they have been at the restaurant for about four hours, one of them actually gets hungry and orders one entrée. The meal comes out to the table. They request more plates so they can share the one entree. Oh, and more refills. And a little more free bread too.

At some point around 4pm, there is a shift change—lunch is over. Day shift servers have counted their money. They have completed their sidework. They are ready to leave for the day. Other servers have come in for the evening shift to take their places. However, Table 2 server is still there on a double-shift, naturally frustrated that the party at Table 2 is still seated at Table 2.

Dinner has a completely different vibration than lunch. The restaurant becomes superbusy for dinner. Everything changes. There are new servers, new guests for dinner. People are drinking alcohol. There is greater laughter. Conversations are louder. The sun has set. The ambiance has changed. Everything is different, except at Table 2, where everything remains the same. The same four black women, eating free bread and requesting free refills on carbonated beverages and iced tea.

Not only did the four black women at Table 2 stay all day, they sat at Table 2 all night. They drank free refills and kept requesting free bread. One of them took a nap. They took turns going to potty, only to return right back and plop down at Table 2. Shamelessly, they sat there while servers wiped and swept up around them, until the ambience faded, until the music stopped and the house lights came on. They had been the very first to show up that morning, and they were the very last four people to walk out of the restaurant. After they left, the restaurant doors were locked...and the staff went berserk.

Servers who had nothing to do with Table 2 were just as pissed as Table 2 server. Dinner servers had watched the ladies occupy the table throughout the entire evening, completely unaware that the ladies had been there through the entire lunch shift as well. Upon learning they had been there from open to close, the servers were flabbergasted. Even the managers were livid. Poor Table 2 server was so frustrated, she was in tears. All in all, the group spent about $40 and left Table 2 server no tip--after having occupied one of her tables for 12 hours.

Table 2 Server only had three tables in her section. When one party occupies one of her three tables for 12 hours without tipping her at all, she is obviously losing lots of money. In that 12-hour period, seven or eight different parties could have come and gone and eaten and tipped her at that very same table. Again, time is money.

As surprising as this may sound, black people do this all the time. Perhaps not always to this 12-hour extreme, but we tend to linger when we dine out while remaining completely apathetic and somewhat selfish about the length of our stay. In reality, a table can overstay its welcome to a point of offense and disrespect.

Servers expect and understand an occasional lengthy visit. Some people are out celebrating. Others may be catching up over a reunion dinner. It is never a server's intention (well, it *should* never be) to move tables quickly in and out, just to make more money. However, sitting at a table for too long without ordering food and/or without compensating the server for the extended table time will ultimately result in a significant loss of wages for that server. Chop chop.

STUFF ON THE TABLE

DO understand the table setting.

Most fine dining establishments preset their tables before you arrive. The napkin, silverware, and sometimes even the wine and water glasses, are already on the table when you are seated.

There are two forks on the table because it is expected that you will start by ordering a salad, an appetizer or a starter course before having an entrée. The second fork is for the actual entrée itself. If there are two knives, it is most likely that one is a salad knife and the other is a steak knife.

Many black people do not know the difference between a salad fork and a dinner fork or which glass is for what. The table settings of some very upscale restaurants can be so immaculate and have so much stuff on the table—it can be quite confusing. As a general rule of dining etiquette, there is clean dinnerware and fresh silverware for each course served. This is why there is more than one fork and sometimes so much stuff on the table.

Although the world won't stop spinning if you use the wrong silverware for each course, understanding the purpose of the silverware would help foster a more pleasant experience.

Many times, when attempting to clear dirty dishes and used silverware from a table of black folks, a guest will snatch his fork off the plate before the server walks away, then look at the server like some sort of mistake was made. The guest might even say, "Hey, you took my fork." However, there is no need to hold on to the dirty silverware. You do not have to wipe off the dirty silverware with your napkin so you can use it again. If the clean fork for the next course was not preset and already on the table, the server knows to bring a clean fork for you for your next course.

To minimize the table setting perplexity, it would be wise to learn more about the stuff on the table. Learn the purpose of the silverware and how to use it properly. Know which glass is for what. An elevated understanding of the purpose of each piece of tableware empowers the guest to better appreciate the entire dining experience.

DON'T pass your plate.

A server approaches a table at various times throughout the meal for different reasons. For instance, if a server walks up to the table to refill everyone's water, let her do that. When a server walks up to your table, it does not mean you can just start handing him stuff. Do not blindly pass empty plates and glasses to that person. Please do not pick up your plate and force it on your server, especially when his hands are already busy.

First of all, if the server only has one free hand, she cannot safely or effectively do very much with that. Secondly, it is unsanitary to carry the clean water pitcher and the dirty plates at the same time. When you are finished eating a particular course, please be patient. Try not to panic.

Some restaurants train servers to clear each dish as soon as the guest is finished with it. Other restaurants train servers to wait until everyone in the party is finished with the course before removing a single dish, as some believe it to be rude to remove one person's plate while another is still eating. Some establishments believe it is proper to wait and clear all the dishes from one course at one time. No need for you, as the guest, to try to control the flow. Your capable server will clear your plates and all dishware at the appropriate time.

WINE SERVICE

DON'T front.

The subject of wine is extremely complex. It takes years of study for a great sommelier or connoisseur to fully understand the varietals and the regions and climates in which they grow. There is so much to understand about enjoying wine. Just looking over a wine list can be intimidating. No one in the restaurant expects that guests who dine there will be privy to all this knowledge. So, it is okay if you do not fully understand the wine list. It is okay if you do not know much about wine at all. It is NOT okay, however, to front and pretend like you know about wine when you have no wine knowledge at all. It just makes you look foolish.

Amidst our insecurity and anxiety over what we do not understand, black folks often suffer ridicule simply from the unwillingness to admit we do not understand. Often when we choose to drink wine, we decide what to order based on how much it costs. We do not consider the winemaker nor the region, and we pay no regard for the year the wine was harvested. We are clueless about how to properly taste the wine, and we just gulp it down when it is sat on the table, never appreciating the value of how the wine was made or where it came from.

A bottle of wine is not just a bottle of wine. Specially selected grapes have been picked and pressed, from which juices have been marinating in a sealed receptacle for years. There is something magical about opening it up to discover what's inside.

There is an entire wine service method in which servers are trained to present this bottled gift to restaurant guests. Servers are taught to carry the wine bottle through the restaurant a certain way, to present the wine to the guest in a certain way. This process maximizes the total wine experience. It's all out of respect for the wine, for the wonder in the patience of waiting on the grape juice to mature into something fantastic. Many of us have no clue that, when we order wine, something special is taking place. We do not understand that there is a high level of respect for the wine or that the server has put on a show in the presentation of the wine. Because we have not taken the time to investigate or research wine, we have no clear understanding of what to do with it. Because of this, black folks are missing out on the beauty of the culture of wine.

Amidst our ignorance, we make impractical moves. Black folks often order wine with an air of sophistication, then proceed to mispronounce the varietal or the label. Or, we will demand a tub of ice for a bottle of red wine, ignorant of the fact that red wine is never served cold.

Don't be intimidated by the wine list. It is perfectly fine that we do not completely understand how the intricacies of wine work. Allow your knowledgeable server, who has been trained to understand the wine list, to guide you through the decision process and help you discover a flavor you will enjoy.

Your server can also bring you a small sample of wine and allow you to taste it before making a decision. Just don't overdo it. Don't sample your server to death. Please keep your request for samples of wine to a respectful minimum. Asking for two samples is decent. Three is pushing it. Four or more—you're doing way too much.

By listening to the server, you can ultimately increase your own wine knowledge a little more with each dining experience. Ultimately, you will be able to order wine you truly love, without mispronunciation, without embarrassment, without the need to front like you know what you are talking about.

DO taste the wine.

There are some important basic steps to enjoying wine. Many wine aficionados take wine tasting to a level far beyond the basic steps, yet most would agree that the following are most important. As a matter of fact, the shape of the wine glass is specifically designed for these things to take place, (Domine, 2000). This is also why there are different wine glasses for different types of wine. Each glass compliments the aerated flavors and helps to balance the components of the corresponding wine, (Domine, 2000).

SEE

First, you should actually see the wine. Take a good look at it. When presented with a glass, first note the color of its contents. The color of the wine is to be appreciated first, as the color provides information to the beholder right away. White wines can range from completely translucent to golden yellow to pale green in color. The color gives us clues regarding the wine's origin. From the wine's color, we gain hints about what type of grape it is, what type of climate it grew in and even possibly the age of the wine (NCWine.org, 2016).

SWIRL

When presented with a taste of wine or a glass of wine, it is customary to first gently swirl the wine around in the glass for a few seconds. The shape of the wine glass is also perfect for swirling the wine without spilling it. The wine is swirled in the glass to aerate the flavors which have been trapped in the bottled for so long. After the swirled wine is aerated, its smells are intensified, and its flavors are more powerful to the palate, (NCWine.org, 2016).

SNIFF

After the wine is swirled, bring the glass up to the nose and smell the aroma of the wine. The wide rim of the wine glass is perfect for poking in one's nose. The circular shape of the wine glass holds the aroma in a whirlpool of sorts, allowing the drinker to savor the flavors marinating inside. Hence, red wine glasses are bigger because red wine flavors are bolder and need more room to allow the flavors to surface (WineEnthusiast.com, 2016). The wine could smell floral or grassy, fruity or smoky. There may be hints of cherry, orange, apple, or spices such as vanilla or cinnamon.

SIP

Now that you have allowed the magnificent flavors of wine to permeate your nasal passageways, you may enjoy a sip. Please do not gulp the wine down. The wine is sipped so that the flavors are introduced to the taste buds in such a way they can be experienced to their fullest potential, (NCWine.org, 2016). Savor the flavors oozing out of the wine. You may taste flavors akin to berries, licorice, pepper or chocolate.

A true wine expert may even go a step further with the tasting. After sipping, he might swish the wine around in the mouth, and let it roll around the tongue. This allows the taste buds to truly savor the flavor of the wine. The sipper can feel the texture of the wine and take note of its lingering aftertaste. Nevertheless, whether you swish or swirl is not as important as making sure you appreciate the wine, and it is difficult to do that with one big gulp.

When you choose to venture out to a fancy shindig for dinner, there is no need to put on airs. This applies not just to the knowledge of wine but to the entire experience. Many restaurants use words from foreign languages to describe their food. This is because most of the dishes are inspired from European cultures and distant lands.

The same is true with wine. The largest wine regions are in France and Italy, so the names of the wines reflect the languages of those foreign lands. It is feasible that you may come across something on a menu that is new to you, that you may have never heard of before. It's okay. If there is something on the menu you do not understand, or if there are words you cannot pronounce, simply ask the server for assistance. No one expects you to become someone you are not just because you go out to eat at a really nice place. It is okay to allow yourself to learn something new, to become a greater version of yourself by being open to what a new experience can teach you.

LARGE PARTIES

DON'T bumrush. DON'T gangbang.

Serving a large party of black folks is one of the best examples of the worst behavior that can be witnessed in a restaurant. During an event such as this, the very worst of all negro cultural proclivity takes place. Meaning, when we dine out in numbers, we show our ass in unbelievable, unforgettable, book-inspiring ways. While serving a large party of black folks, every negative stereotype of black people can be witnessed in just one seemingly simple dinner.

Whenever a restaurant is expecting a party of 10 or more, you can most likely bet that it will be black folks. No other group of people gathers in such large numbers so often. So, what's the big deal? What's wrong with a party of 10? Well, nothing...when the party is considerate and kind. However, when you consider all the issues black diners bring to the table individually, a group of 10 can be too much to handle. Besides, many fancy restaurants do not accommodate parties this large, unless they've reserved a private room. Often times, black folks will just show up willy-nilly with a large party like this, and then they become pissed off and racially charged when the restaurant cannot accommodate them. Fact is, the restaurant may have no space and no efficient way to oblige such a large party with no advance notice. Please try to keep the number of seats in your party under ten. Any party of such size should always first make a reservation and perhaps request a private section.

DON'T come out to celebrate, if you are not going to actually celebrate.

A restaurant can be the perfect place to enjoy a celebration. There are times when black folks *do* actually make a proper reservation for a group to celebrate a birthday, engagement or graduation. The restaurant will go above and beyond to accommodate the large group...and then only half the people show up.

If you make a reservation for a party of 20, and only 8 people show, the 12 empty seats will create problems for everyone involved. First of all, it dampens the mood of the celebration, which can potentially last throughout the entire visit. Secondly, it becomes a huge waste of time, energy and money for the server and the restaurant.

The same is true if 20 people *do* actually show up, but only 8 people order food. If 20 people are gathered around a table and only 8 of them are eating and drinking, it diminishes the celebration drastically. The folks who didn't order food are just sitting around, taking up space and feeling uncomfortable. It is counterproductive and awkward for everyone—including the server. If you are going out to celebrate with a loved one, let loose. Drop the dough and celebrate for real.

DON'T be late for someone else's surprise.

If your party is coming together for a surprise gathering, it is proper for all the guests to show up before the guest of honor. In this scenario, the entire party should already be seated and waiting on that special person to arrive. Otherwise, it becomes a compete catastrophe—staggering, tardy arrivals and impatient guests who want to order food without waiting on the entire group to arrive.

Instead of everyone eating and drinking and sharing together, people are trickling in at all different times throughout the gathering. Two or three folks in the party are already eating. Another two are just placing their orders. Two or three more are just arriving and sitting down. The server has to keep repeating the features and answering the same menu questions over and over again, while running back and forth for food and drinks and more entrées.

It is a celebration for togetherness, yet everyone is one a different page, doing something different. There is no synergy in the celebration. Amidst all the unsynchronized movement, the mood is more akin to a church pot luck or a backyard barbeque than a surprise celebration at a fancy shindig. Show up correctly.

DO offer cake to your server.
Most restaurants welcome the cutting of a special cake among guests. Please understand, however, that some fine dining establishments require patrons to pay a fee for the storage of dessert brought in from some other place. Others have a cutting fee, which can cost up to $3 per person. Essentially, the restaurant is saying:

> *Hey, we'll let you bring in cake from somewhere else, but we'll charge you fees equivalent to the price of our own cake.*

Whether or not this is fair, it is arguable.

Nobody wants to be a party pooper and rain on someone's parade by giving them issues about a birthday cake. However, from a service standpoint, cake can be a pain in the ass. First of all, here is a guest that has purchased cake from somewhere else and is bringing this cake into a restaurant that actually serves its own cake. It's like bringing sand to the beach. Then the guest is requesting that this outside-bought cake be stored or refrigerated in the restaurant cooler—next to the in-house cake that the restaurant sells. When the time is right, the server must fetch this cake, de-box it, add candles and fire to it and attempt to walk it out to the table without losing a light. Before this is done, the server must seek out and provide plates and silverware and a special cake knife from the restaurant kitchen. And in most cases, the server is expected to cut the cake and plate it as well.

Of course, the server is there to satisfy every need the guest may have. However, many guests view cake service as an automatic expectation and demand all these details without even so much as offering the server a piece of cake afterward. Even worse, they do not tip the server to show appreciation and gratitude for all the extra work involved in helping make the celebration dinner a success. And to top it all off, the mess that cake leaves on a table of a party of grown-ups requires the same cleaning needed for cake on a table of a party of toddlers. Icing all over the table. Cake all over the floor. Crumbs in all the seats. Half-eaten cake on a plate next to chewed up gum. It is a sticky, colorful hot mess. The only thing worse than cleaning it up...is not getting tipped for it...and not being offered a piece. After all the work the server put into serving the cake, the least a party can do is be thoughtful enough to offer a piece. Just know that the piece of cake is *in addition to* the tip and is not the tip itself.

VOLUME

DON'T be loud.

There is a time and place for everything. There is a time to be loud and a time for peace. Dinner is not the time, and the restaurant is not the place for loudness, screaming or yelling. It is impolite to impose on the quiet joy of others around you.

Black folks are colorful, lively, passionate people. We do not attempt to contain our emotions, especially happiness and laughter. As a general rule in life, this is a wonderful attribute to behold. To live life, laughing out loud, is an enviable ideal. In a restaurant environment, however, life is enjoyed with respect to others with whom the atmosphere is shared. Your freedom of volume ends where the next table's freedom of quiet begins.

Other guests are often offended by the inappropriately loud conversation and outright bursts of laughter. They feel encroached upon enough to stop a server and ask the server to ask the loud, black people to please not be so disturbing to others around them. We seem clueless about how loud we can be. Somehow, we do not seem to be able to differentiate between club behavior and that of elegant dining.

Sometimes we are simply caught up in having a great time. Out having a wonderful night, reminiscing with friends and family, it is easy to get carried away with loudness and laughter. Other times, it appears we simply do not care. In this regard, we are often shamelessly inconsiderate of other people. We will share a ghetto story, loud enough for the entire restaurant to hear it. Black folks will make an extremely loud personal phone call, right at the table, in the middle of a group conversation. Black folks will share online videos at the dinner table with the volume all the way up to sky-high. We will even allow our children to play video games on tablets and cell phones, with no headphones, no discipline, no regard to the volume at all. None of this should take place in a nice restaurant setting.

The last thing a server wants to do is walk up to a group of happy black folks and tell them they are too loud, to tell them they are disturbing the guests around them. A group of loud, happy black folks can be quite intimidating, even to another black person. It's like starting a war with a group of angry soldiers who are already looking for a fight. Most often, this approach will lead to further complications. As black folks don't like to be told what to do, asking them to decrease their volume will only fuel the fire of complaints and give black folks reason to act ignorant and feel completely justified. Asking a group of black folks to turn down their volume almost always results in the involvement of a manager, the addition of complimentary food and/or the removal of something off the bill.

The truth of the matter is: black people can be quite loud. No one wants to risk starting a war with black folks by telling them they are too loud. So, if someone has mustered up the courage it takes to approach you and ask you to turn down, your volume is most likely way too high. You should check yourself, rather than get mad and get even louder.

And please get off the phone, and try to live in the moment.

CHILDREN

DO discipline your children. DO teach them how to behave properly. Children look to their parents and caregivers for guidance on how to do things in life. Our children mock our every behavior, including the restaurant etiquette we exhibit or the lack thereof. It is crucial that black folks teach their children how to properly dine in a restaurant. This cannot be achieved by simply taking children out to eat. They must be disciplined and proactively taught the difference between what is proper and what is completely unacceptable. Otherwise, they will grow up and mimic the same behavior at restaurants they witnessed from their parents.

When parents bring their children along to a restaurant, they must be disciplined. It is not okay for your children to be out of their seats, running back and forth across the restaurant floor. When children are ripping through the restaurant, it creates a dangerous environment for the wait staff to wade through. More importantly, your children can get hurt. Many times, when children are out of their seats, they get knocked to the floor by runners and bussers carrying heavy plates and trays who simply do not see nor expect the small children in their path.

Also, please do not allow your children to throw food all over the table and all over the floor. Don't let them tear up paper and throw it everywhere. Most servers from fine dining establishments have been trained how to handle children and what to offer them to help keep them calm and happy when they visit with their families. It would be wise to implore the server for help in keeping your children delightfully occupied. Consequently, if you know your child/ren required extra attention, feel free to leave your server a worthy tip—to thank them for going the extra mile to care for your kids *and* for having to clean up the disaster they leave behind.

It is clear that we have not trained our children how to dine out. It is impossible to teach them how to behave if we, ourselves, do not even understand. Every year, in the middle of the spring, groups of prom-bound teenagers and high school graduates venture out into nice restaurants all across the country, wreaking havoc on everybody employed in the restaurant. They go out alone, without adult supervision, without any knowledge whatsoever about how to enjoy the experience. It is quite shameful. Serving them can be a nightmare.

The way these young people behave is a direct result of how their parents behave. Their childhood memories of how their parents behaved in a restaurant is the only point of reference they have. If they watched their parents be disrespectful and dismissive to the waitstaff, they will do the same thing when they are old enough to go out alone. If they witnessed their parents order things and then send them back, they will do the same. If they see their parents trying to get stuff for free, so will they. If they witnessed their parents walking out without tipping, they will do the same. If you are out dining with your children, correct them on the spot when they make mistakes, when they are impolite or unmannerable. Get cozy with the proper etiquette for dining. Then, reiterate these lessons to your children. Teach them how to treat others by setting the example as the loving parent who wants them to appreciate, rather than diminish, the world in which they live.

PRETTY LIL LIARS

I will never forget the party of teenagers who came in to celebrate this one girl's 16th birthday. It was one of the worst serving experiences I've ever had.

The evening kicked off with the usual signs of impending wretchedness. The group sashayed in—all dressed up, incomplete party, late for their reservation and requesting more seats. They had made a reservation for 8 but had invited about 20 people.

The service began in a chaotic state with me running around with bussers and management attempting to create more space for people who weren't even at the restaurant yet. We ended up splitting the party into two adjacent sections. Twelve seats were at my table, then the other eight would go in the other section with another server. Because all the guests had not yet arrived, there were only about four or five at my table—all teens. The other server only had two people—the birthday girl's mother and a girlfriend she had brought along.

Once the incomplete party was seated, they did not want to wait for the latecomers. They wanted to start ordering right away. While walking the young teens through the menu, it was obvious that they had very little money by the questions they asked and the way they chose to order. As I circled the table to take their orders, I watched and took notes as they debated over water vs. lemonade and who would share what with whom.

After asking whether or not it came with free refills, one brave soul was bold enough to place an order for lemonade. Everyone else ordered water with straws. When I returned with the waters and the single awesome-looking, freshly-squeezed lemonade, the group bellowed out in unison, "Ooooo." Now three or four of the other kids wanted lemonade too. I fetched more awesome-looking, freshly-squeezed lemonade. They finally decided what they wanted to eat, and I brought out the stuff they ordered. They ate. More friends showed up. They ordered. More friends showed up.

They didn't order anything, just wanted water. More appetizers arrived for the latecomers, while others were demanding dessert.

By the time the numbers were counted, there ended up being 15 kids at my 12-seat table. Turns out, no one wanted to sit with mama and homegirl. Instead, they took chairs from nearby tables and crammed all 15 of themselves into my section.

As dinner finally reached its ending, I split the bill for all of the kids and passed checks out to them. Out of 15 kids, only two of them paid their bills uncontested, without problem. Earlier, two of the young ladies had spent several minutes debating whether or not to share a grilled shrimp appetizer. One of these girls had convinced the other to go ahead and try the dish, and they had agreed to split the cost of the appetizer. Now, at cash cough-up time, these same two girls were denying that they ate the shrimp appetizer, claiming that the shrimp never even made it to the table.

Perhaps they figured that I did not remember checking on the two of them while they were enjoying the grilled shrimp appetizer, to make sure they liked it. Because one of them was so skeptical about ordering the shrimp in the first place, I had made certain to ask her, while she was eating it, if she liked it. She had replied, "yes," and said she was glad they ordered it. Now that it was time to pay, suddenly we were all in a parallel universe where the shrimp never made it to the table.

After witnessing the shrimp ordeal from her seat across the table, another girl decided that she did not like her dessert and asked that it be "taken off" her bill. This created a chain reaction among the others. Suddenly, four more ladies each said that they did not like their desserts either. Interestingly, they all had ordered different desserts. No other guest in the entire restaurant had a problem with the desserts served that evening. However, at this table, all the desserts were garbage.

It was clear that each girl had been struck with the epiphany that you could just tell the server that you didn't like the dish to get it for free, rather than go through the extravagance of lying and swearing that you never received it. After this, two of the others claimed that they did not order lemonade. As this was not my first rodeo, I completely understood what was happening.

To help ease the situation, I removed the garbage desserts and the mysterious lemonades from each of their bills. I had hoped this would expedite their departure. However, even after removing these items from their checks, several of them still did not have enough cash to cover their bills. Instead of going to get a manager, I went straight to go get birthday girl's mama.

During the entire dinner, birthday girl's mama had not been over to visit birthday girl's table at all. By this time, her homegirl was gone and she was the lone adult, half ass chaperoning these literal crumb-snatchers. She agreed that she would talk to the group and resolve the issues regarding all the discrepancies over the bills. She seemed sensible and intelligent, and I was relieved that I had spoken to her. However, when I returned to discuss the outcome with her, she simply repeated back to me all of the same grievances the children had given. She started our conversation off a little something like this:

Mama: *Well, they said they never got the shrimp.*

Me: *Oh, they got the shrimp. Not only did they get the shrimp, but I watched them argue over whether or not to order it. Then I checked on them while they were eating it to make sure they liked it, after which I cleared the empty dish from the table.*

Mama: *Well, why would they lie?*

Me: *Well, apparently none of them have enough money to pay these bills. I mean, what are the odds that more than half of them are trying to get things for free? I have spent a*

> *lot of time and energy giving them excellent service ma'am, and it's obvious that I'm already not going to be tipped for my time and effort. I need for them to at least pay these bills.*

This shit went on forever. I went back and forth between birthday girl's mama and the rest of the kids and my managers, attempting to void and comp miscellaneous items, settle debts and collect cash. Before the catastrophe was settled, birthday girl's mama had to pull out her credit card to close out some of the bills for these kids. I still ended up about $15 short in cash and had no money left for tips. I had spent almost three hours taking care of them.

Birthday girl's mama, after all that drama from all those thieving children, tipped me $5 on her credit card.

TO GO BOXES

DON'T request a to-go box for two bites of food.

Please...just let it go.

PAYMENT

DON'T question a correct bill.

It seems the only time you can get a group of loud black folks to quiet down is to drop the bill on the table. Obnoxiously inconsiderate volume comes to a screeching halt of silence once they receive the bill for the food. The air around them becomes filled with deliberate contemplation and muffled anxiety. Boisterous laughter is replaced with insecurity, hesitation and skepticism. It is time to pay. Drumroll please.

It is rare for a black person to hand his payment over to the server without a microscopic investigation of the itemized receipt. Black folks study the restaurant bill like it's a paycheck stub. Then they summons the server over to the table to explain every item on the bill, only to be reminded that they did actually order that appetizer and ate it. Servers have to help them remember that they ordered and drank three drinks when they somehow only remember having two. They don't remember the prices being so high, so they ask the server to bring the menu back to the table to confirm they were charged the correct price on the bill. The sudden memory loss is incredible. It is as if when the bill hits the table, it casts a mysterious spell of restaurant amnesia, whereby everyone needs hypnosis to remember what happened in the last two hours.

However, there is no real memory loss here. Our deepest fears about money and spending manifest themselves in these ridiculous ways. We investigate. We challenge. We manipulate the situation in order to decrease the bill to a number with which our conscious can be comfortable. It quells our fears a bit and temporarily throws the money monkey off our backs.

Customers who are comfortable spending money do not hesitate to pay the bill. When it is time to pay, this customer drops his card on the table without even once looking at the receipt. When that customer steps foot into the restaurant, he is trusting. Great food and great service are expected. To him, the server is knowledgeable and capable...and trustworthy. Part of understanding great service includes trusting that the server rang up the bill correctly and double-checked it to ensure its accuracy before delivering it to the table. There is no fuss. There is no questioning. There is no worrying about the incidentals. There is no drumroll. There is no amnesia.

It is self-defeating to endeavor to have a great time, then fret over the money you spent to make it happen. Just like with the to-go boxes, we must learn to let go of the constant need to challenge and manipulate these situations. It just fosters unnecessary stress and stands in the way of our very own happiness.

If you do find an error on your bill, it is not an opportunity to be self-righteous or rude. Mistakes can easily happen, especially serving black folks who almost always create confusion in this environment. It is the way we handle, the way we communicate the mistakes that makes the difference in the outcome of the situation. If you do indeed notice an error on your bill, politely notify the server who will, with apology, correct the mistake right away. However, if the bill is correct, just pay the damn bill.

DO treat each other more often.
Two or three individuals decide to have lunch or dinner together. Each would like to pay separately. No problem. All types and kinds and races of people request to split the check and separate the bill. With black folks, however, the notion of splitting a check turns into something much more outrageous. Twenty black people will split a bill 19 different ways, then demand they are in a hurry to leave. Then, many of them will use their impatience with processing the bill as an excuse to leave a substandard tip.

Black folks need to split the check—always. No matter the size of the party—two people or ten—we always request to have the bill dissected to split the check. The fact that we constantly request that the bill be split up into segments symbolizes a deeper disharmony at the table. No one is treating—ever. With the exception of couples or families who usually share one bill, black folks are not at all inclined to treat each other. The undertone of the continuous request to split the check clearly identifies that we will only be responsible for our own selves.

Many times, a black party will inform the server that there will be separate checks before they have even had the opportunity to order their drinks. Making sure we are not charged for the requests of others in our party trumps everything else in importance, and we want to make it perfectly clear—from the absolute start—that we are not paying for anybody else's meal.

The *I pay my way, you pay yours* mentality is the opposite of black people's inherent capacity for love and community. It promotes a preoccupation with only supporting one's own self without regard or consideration for another. It stops us from reaching out. It prevents us from creating an experience in such a way so as to make someone else's day. Amidst our self-preoccupation, we have lost our natural inclination to make someone else happy.

If you have requested that the bill be split up multiple ways, please be patient with your server. It takes an extra amount of time to divide bills into several different checks. In order for the server to split the checks accurately without error and keep up with all the paperwork involved, it may take a few extra minutes, especially if you have had dishes returned and need items removed from the bill.

Comping items requires the involvement of a manager. Your server must first attempt to locate a manager, who is already prioritizing issues and may be unavailable or simply missing in action or on smoke break. Your server must complete this complicated task for you while simultaneously providing excellent service to other guests. To make matters even more difficult, some point-of-sale systems are less savvy than others when it comes to making these types of changes. Some systems will even shut down from running too many payments back-to-back this way. The printer may run out of paper in the middle of printing. It may require an unbelievable amount of extra time to process a split check request, due to no fault of your server. Extraordinary measures call for extraordinary time.

Have more consideration for your server. And certainly, be more thoughtful of those with whom you dine. Dare yourself to be kind enough to pay someone else's bill.

DO read the fine print.

Before you go out to the fine restaurant of your choice with your promotional discount or coupon, please be sure to read entirely the specifications of your discount card or document. Black folks go out to dine with a promotion they found on the internet without reading the details of the promotion. For some reason, we only read the big print. The promotion could be only available on certain days or during certain hours, or even expired, but because we did not read the entire promotion, we show up and try to use it at the wrong time. The same with gift cards. We show up with gift cards, but we don't verify the balance or validity beforehand. This creates confusion and embarrassing complications.

> "Oh, we didn't know."
> "Oh, we didn't see it."

When we do not read the fine print, we end up sitting at the table in surprise when it's bill time.

We only came prepared to spend a certain amount and we were dependent on the discount to cover the remainder. Without the use of the gift card that we did not check or the promotion we did not read, we do not have enough money to cover the bill. So, now what? Again, this is the point where we expect the restaurant to make an exception on our behalf or do something special to compensate our ignorance. And we have the nerve to get upset if the restaurant does not or is not able to submit to our demands, when we were the ones who did not read the particulars. These situations are unnecessary and completely avoidable, if we would simply take a little time to read.

DON'T round off.
Please do not base a tip off of your personal need to balance your total with double zeroes. Some left-brained individuals prefer to always total a bill, so that the complete tab is a nice, round whole number...like $57.00. Some diners are obsessed with making sure everything adds up to double zeros on the end.

For example, a customer's pre-tip bill is $26.79. At 20 percent tip, this customer owes the server $5.34. However, when it's time to pay, he just leaves an even $30.00. He loves whole numbers. Because of his obsession with the zeroes, the server only receives $3.21—a little more than half of what he should receive. Please refrain from this practice if it means jilting a deserving waiter. Or, of course, if you absolutely must see the zeroes, then make sure you round *up* the total for your server to receive more than 20 percent, not less.

DO pay your entire bill.
One would think one would not have to explain to others to...pay the bill. It is the most basic of knowledge that when you dine out at a restaurant, you must pay the bill—the entire bill. However, this may not be absolutely clear to some black folks.

Sometimes, when paying with cash, black folks don't even leave enough money to pay for the total balance on the receipt. This is irrespective of leaving a tip. Some black folks leave cash on the table and leave the restaurant in a hurry, only for the server to discover after their departure that they did not leave enough money to pay the bill, much less a penny to tip the server for his service. Some black folks actually think it is okay to pay the bill and be two or three or five dollars short. When there is not enough cash left to cover the cost of the bill, that cash must come out of that server's pocket. In essence, the server has served you for free *and* paid a small portion of your bill. This behavior is unacceptable. It is disingenuous, dishonest and disrespectful.

If you find you do not have enough money to pay your bill—*which should never happen*, have a conversation with your server or with the manager. In the absence of an ATM machine or some other way to get money quickly, talk to someone. Communicate the issue. Politely explain the situation, and apologize for the inconvenience. Then, return to the restaurant at a very near future date to settle your balance and leave a generous tip for the server who had to pay the balance of your bill from his pocket on the day you dined out and couldn't pay your entire bill. Do the right thing.

DO keep the change.

Servers, just like church pastors, have no interest in coin change. They, too, want the kind of money that folds, not the kind that jingles. Silent, noiseless money. Paper Abe, not copper-plated Abe. Coin change is a nuisance to carry around and tedious to keep up with. And to servers, coin change as part of a tip is considered insulting. No change. No thanks.

FINAL WORD

Learning how to tip properly is all fine and dandy. However, it doesn't matter if a patron is a great tipper, if he is inconsiderate and disrespectful to the server. Tipping is definitely about money, but it is more about respect. There is a direct correlation between tipping and respect. Most times, the people who do not tip properly are the same people who are thoughtless, discourteous and disrespectful. Hence, understanding how to tip properly involves an open-hearted willingness to be kind to other people.

Kindness, caring, respect and generosity all fall under the umbrella of love. As the world continues to look to African-American culture for the recipes for equality, justice, beauty and excellence, we must more readily embrace and practice these notions of love...so we can show the rest of the world how to be the best of themselves. As black people elevate higher and higher into the frequencies of love, the rest of the world will begin to know us for the extraordinary people we truly are, as they follow suit and do the same.

WORKS CITED

Adams, Susan. "What Kids in 2015 Want to be When They Grow Up." *Forbes*, 14 Dec 2015. Web. Feb 2019.

Akbari, Cherine. "Four Arrested After Restaurant Brawl Injures Waiter in Coral Springs." *NBCMiami*, 15 Dec 2014. Web. May 2016.

Angyal, Chloe. "The American Restaurant Industry is Number One for Sexual Harassment Claims." *Feministing*, 2015. Web. Aug 2016.

Artz, Liz. "Restaurant Fight." *WSB-TV Atlanta*. Youtube, 10 May 2016. Web. May 2016.

Barnes, Harry Elmer. "Historical Origin of the Prison System in America." *Journal of Criminal Law and Criminology* 12.1 (1921): Article 5. Print.

Bornstein, Kate. *Gender Outlaw*. New York: Vintage Books, 1995. Print.

Bourdain, Anthony. *Kitchen Confidential*. New York: HarperCollins, 2007. Print.

Brenner, Brad. "Understanding Anxiety and Depression for LGBTQ People." ADAA.org, n.d. Web. Oct 2019.

Coke, Marguerite M., and James A. Twaite. *The Black Elderly*. New York: The Haworth Press, 1995. Print.

Deluca, Gina L. *The Menu*. Wiser Waitress, 2010. Web. Mar 2015.

"The Difference Between Red and White Wine Glasses." WineEnthusiast, 2016. Web. Jan 2016.

Dolak, Kevin. "Applebee's Fires Waitress Who Posted Nontipping Pastor's Check Online." *Good Morning American and World News*. ABCNews, 1 Feb 2013. Web. Jan 2016.

Domine, Andre, Eckhard Supp, and Dunja Ulbricht. "A History of Enjoying Wine." *Wine*. Konemann Verlagsgesellschaft mbH, 2000. 8–75. Print.

WORKS CITED

"Dram Shop Civil Liability and Criminal Penalty State Statutes." National Conference of State Legislatures. NCSL, 14 Jun 2013. Web. Dec 2016.

Dublanica, Steve. *Keep the Change*. New York: HarperCollins, 2010. Print.

Dublanica, Steve. *Waiter Rant*. New York: HarperCollins, 2008. Print.

Echlin, Helena. "When Restaurants Refuse Substitutions." *FoodNews*. Chow.com, 21 Jun 2011. Web. Feb 2015.

Equal Employment Opportunity Commission. *Preventing and Addressing Workplace Harassment*. EEOC, 14 Jan 2015. Web. Aug 2016.

Equal Employment Opportunity Commission. *Sexual Harassment*. EEOC.org, n.d. Web. Aug 2016.

Erb, Kelly Phillips. "Pastor Who Refused to Pay Applebee's Service Charge Becomes Unwitting Poster Child for Server Pay and Tax Issues." *Forbes*. Forbes, 1 Feb 2013. Web. Jan 2016.

Fishbein, Rebecca. "Waitresses With Red Lips Earn More $$$, Says Science." *Food*. Gothamist.com, 12 May 2012. Web. Mar 2017.

"The Five S's of Wine Tasting." *North Carolina Department of Agriculture and Consumer Services*. NCWine, 2016.

Garvey, Michael, Heather Dismore, and Andrew Dismore. *Running a Restaurant for Dummies*. Indianapolis: Wiley Publishing, 2004. Print.

Gerard, Leo. "How the System Favors Corporations Who Break the Rules Over the Working Class." *Alternet*. Alternet, 19 May 2015. Web. Sep 2015.

Giesen, James C. "Sharecropping." *New Georgia Encyclopedia: History and Archaeology—Civil War and Reconstruction, 1861-1877*. NGE, 28 Aug 2019. Web. Dec 2019.

Habersham, Raisa. "Four People Cited in East Point Mother's Day Brawl." *Atlanta Journal Constitution*. AJC, 16 May 2016. Web. May 2016.

Harris, Jenn. "The California Minimum Wage Increase: What It Would Mean for Restaurants and Your Dinner Bill." *DailyDish*. LATimes, Mar 2016. Web. May 2016.

Hernandez, Vittorio. "Study: Waiters Take Average of 23,000 Steps Per Day." *International Business Times*. IBTimes, 3 Apr 2012. Web. Feb 2016.

"History of the Prison System." *The Howard League for Penal Reform*. Howard League, n.d. Web. Jun 2015.

Holt, David L. "What is the Protocol for Tipping? 20 Percent Isn't Too Much." *The Denver Post*. DenverPost, 2 Aug 2013. Web. Mar 2015.

Horsley, Scott. "Spending Bill Protects Tipped Workers From Sharing With The Boss." *The Salt*. Npr.org, 23 Mar 2018. Web. Mar 2019.

"How to Correctly Share Tips (Tip Pooling vs. Tip Sharing)." *Restaurant Tip Laws*. Tipmetric.com, 6 Oct 2017. Web. Mar 2019.

Jayaraman, Saru. *Forked: A New Standard for American Dining*. New York, NY: Oxford University Press, 2016. Print.

Jensen, Hope. "Police Searching for 5 People Involved in Huge Mother's Day Brawl." *WSB-TV Atlanta*. WSBTV, 10 May 2016. Web. May 2016.

Kavoussi, Bonnie. "Foreign Tourists Charged An Automatic Tip at Restaurants in Burlington, Vermont." *The Huffington Post*. Huffington Post, 28 Aug 2012. Web. Mar 2015.

Keller, Bill. "Enron for Dummies." *The New York Times*. NYTimes, 26 Jan 2002. Web. Nov 2014.

Lempert, Phil. "3 Big Reasons the Food Industry Needs Immigrants." *Forbes*. Forbes, 28 Feb 2017. Web. Jan 2019.

WORKS CITED

Lynn, Michael and Zachary Brewster. "What's Behind Racial Differences in Restaurant Tipping." *The Washington Post*. WashingtonPost, 21 Jan 2015. Web. Jun 2016.

Moos, Jeanne. "Pastor Uses Tithe Excuse to Dispute Tip." CNN, 31 Jan 2013. Web. Jan 2016.

Nirappil, Fenit. "It's official: D.C. Council has repealed Initiative 77, which would have raised pay for tipped workers." *The Washington Post*. WashingtonPost, 16 Oct 2018. Web. Jan 2019.

Nirappil, Fenit and Tim Carman. "Tipping the pay scales: Initiative 77 could dramatically alter D.C. restaurant culture." *The Washington Post*. WashingtonPost, 16 Jun 2018. Web. Jan 2019.

O'Grady, Kevin. "Why Does the LGBT Community Experience Such High Levels of Anxiety?" Anxiety.org, 26 Jun 2015. Web. Oct 2019.

Parry, Wynne. "Tip for Waitresses: Wear Red Lipstick." *News*. Livescience.com, 11 May 2012. Web. Mar 2017.

Post, Peggy, et al. *Emily Post's Etiquette—Manners for a New World*. 18th ed. New York: HarperCollins, 2011. Print.

"Prisons in England." *BBC Timeline*. BBC, 7 Apr 2006. Web. Aug 2016.

Ralph, Talia. "How Restaurants Hire Undocumented Workers." *Eater*. Eater, 28 Feb 2017. Web. Jan 2019.

"Religious Landscape Study, 2007." *Pew Research Center*. PewForum, 2016. Web. Jan 2016.

Restaurant Opportunities Center United. ROCU, 2015. Web. Aug 2016.

Rivera, Dick. "A Bad Tip for Restaurant Employees." *The Chicago Tribune*. Chicago Tribune, 25 Apr 2012. Web. Feb 2016.

Scheiber, Noam. "New Labor Department rule would let employers distribute tips more widely." The New York Times. New York Times, 22 Dec 2020. Web. Mar 2021.

Seiden, Michael. "4 Arrested in Brawl at Big Bear Brewing Company." Local 10, 15 Dec 2014. Web. May 2016.

Shallcross, Lynne. "Survey: Half of Food Workers Go To Work Sick Because They Have To." *National Public Radio*. NPR, 19 Oct 2015. Web. Dec 2016.

Strutner, Suzy. "Half of Food Industry Employees Work When They're Sick." *The Huffington Post*. Huffington Post, 20 October 2015. Web. Dec 2016.

"There's Nothing Polite About Declining Modifications and Substitutions." *The Primalist*. ThePrimalist, 10 Apr 2012. Web. Oct 2015.

Westcott, Sam. "Why Waiters Are the Fittest Workers." PRWeb, 16 Jun 2012. Web. Feb 2016.

"Why Shape Matters." *All About Riedel*. Riedel, 2015. Web. Jan 2016.

Zagorsky, Jay. "Is it Time to End Tipping?" *The Wall Street Journal.* WSJ, Feb 2016. Web. May 2016.

ACKNOWLEDGEMENTS

I must testify. It does not usually take most writers 6 years to write a book. It just took *me* 6 years to write this one. As an artist, when you are struck by a golden epiphany to share something with the world, you just do it. The urgency of the divine inspiration simply won't wait. But, then again, sometimes circumstances of life can force a process to take much longer than expected. Money definitely helps expedite the process, but without it, you hold steadfast to your dreams and push forward every day until you reach the top of your mountain.

Though I couldn't always write when I wanted to, I wrote when I could. I wrote in the in-between time, whenever Mommy wasn't needed for something. I wrote after working grueling 14-hour shifts. I wrote in the twinkle of the night when the world was mostly hibernating. I wrote in the early morning before the bustling noises of the new day began. I wrote when I wanted to be out ripping a microphone instead. I wrote on the backs of customer receipts, on torn off scraps from paper bags, on notes in my smartphone. I typed on an outdated computer with a cracked display screen. I wrote through hunger and poverty and food stamps and evictions and disconnections and repossessions and multiple trips to the pawn shop. I wrote in Old Fourth Ward. I wrote Downtown. I wrote in Midtown. I wrote in Buckhead. A moment here, a few moments there, a come-up here, a setback there—all totaling up to 6 years.

No one gives a damn that you are writing a book of true substance that will affect the world. Landlords want their money. Massa wants his slaves at work on time. Baby needs shoes. It seems no one has a care or clue about what it takes to focus on an endeavor of this magnitude. People casually forget that you are writing a book—even though it's all you talk about, even though it's the very air you breathe.

ACKNOWLEDGEMENTS

So, with every fiber in my being, I am most grateful to those who understood and remembered—those who remembered I was writing a book, those who stood by me through the entire ordeal. You have sustained me with encouragement, laughter, shared stories, suggestions, support...and money. You have kept me on track by continuously pushing me forward to the finish line.

First of all and most of all, I thank my daughter, **AlmaRose Sovereign Voice GoldenHeart Teacher**, who is my sweetest inspiration. I know no other world than this one of artistic creation and expression. Thank you, Mommy's baby, for all you have had to sacrifice by being the daughter of a ride or die artist. You are my biggest fan and my greatest joy. No one supports me more than you. What joy that I get to be your Mommy!

To my cousin, **Tynarria Simmons**, thank you so very much for your genuine love and undying support. I am so grateful that we get to share this life journey together. You are the truest, realest definition of family. To **Reese Dillard**, I cannot express in words how much I appreciate your artistic genius and your literary brilliance. Thank you for riding with me on this restaurant roller coaster and for cheering me along the whole way. Your faith in me is cherished more than I can put into words. I also would like to thank **XPJ7** for his constant love and continued support. Your daily reminders of my "literary genius" kept me most humble yet helped me keep my eyes on the prize. Thank you so much for believing in me. **Mariah Littlejohn**, my first partner-in-crime, thank you so much for sharing this restaurant journey with me. The memories we made in those joints will warm my heart always. Forever love you.

Special thanks to **Karen James** for having faith in me and believing in my message. Much love and appreciation to **Robert Flagg** for being a source of love and support in my life since day one. Extremely grateful to **Terry Williams** for always inspiring me to be a better person and encouraging me to be a greater artist.

Thanks to my loving family. Thanks so very much to **Uncle Walter** and **Cousin Virginia** for always calling across the miles to check on me. Thanks to **Cousin Kandi** for loving me so strong and keeping me real. To **Cousin Tasha**, thank you for your heart of gold and for being right there when I call. Eternal thanks to **Aunt Fannie** and **Uncle Larry** for your constant embrace and unconditional love. One love to everyone in my **Jones Fam**, my **Stephens Fam**, my **Jacobs Fam** and my **Simmons Fam**.

I also want to acknowledge the following people who have also inspired me greatly, encouraged me immensely and always lifted me up in love—**Steven "Kwame" Gooden**, **Twin Spirit**, **Ifakemi Spriggs** and the **Spriggs Family** and the **Burr Family**.

To my very special friends—who know me and love me anyway—**Cheiko High** and **Pzoflin Redd**—I hope you realize how much you mean to me. I love you both to the moon.

Much love to **Andrea W. Smith—Word Alignment Specialist,** for helping me proofread and encouraging me forward. Many thanks to Shan Williams and the entire cast and crew who helped make my promotional videos such a success.

The following industry professionals may never have known how much each of them has impacted my life in such a dynamic way. I have never forgotten and will never forget the kindness of each of your hearts, the exceptional ways you looked out for me, and I thank you eternally for being a sense of calm in the middle of my storm: **Julie Badger**, **Kevin Krapp**, **Toby Franklin**, **Rufus Murray**, **Lydia Dull** and **Greg Lofton**.

And finally...to every wonderful human being I've had the pleasure of serving with, thank you for the unforgettable memories. I honor you and lift you up high.

www.ingramcontent.com/pod-product-compliance
Lightning Source LLC
Chambersburg PA
CBHW070812270326
41927CB00010B/2383

* 9 7 8 0 9 7 0 0 9 0 6 1 4 *